James J. Dowd

James J. Dowd
Department of Sociology]

To Jim!
with warm regards,
Fred Katz

Consulting Editor: DENNIS H. WRONG, NEW YORK UNIVERSITY

AUTONOMY and ORGANIZATION

The Limits of Social Control

Fred E. Katz   STATE UNIVERSITY OF NEW YORK AT BUFFALO

RANDOM HOUSE / NEW YORK

FIRST PRINTING

© Copyright, 1968, by Random House, Inc.

All rights reserved under International and Pan-American Copyright Conventions.
Published in New York by Random House, Inc. and simultaneously in Toronto,
Canada, by Random House of Canada Limited.

Library of Congress Catalog Card Number: 68–13468

Manufactured in the United States of America by The Colonial Press Inc.

Design by Diana Hrisinko

TO Hertha Karger
She has contributed to the
autonomy of many persons.

Acknowledgments

This book began over a discussion of modern education, while I taught at the University of Missouri. It evolved as I began to see that autonomy can be considered an ingredient of social structures. I should like to thank the persons who contributed to this thought process. I am particularly indebted to Bruce Biddle, Paul Rosenblatt, and Clyde Wilson. I should also like to take this opportunity to thank some of my teachers who have, in many ways, contributed to my development: David Stafford, who introduced me to sociology, and Frederick Crownfield, who introduced me to A. N. Whitehead, both at Guilford College; my teachers at the University of North Carolina at Chapel Hill, especially William Noland, Rupert Vance, Guy Johnson, Katherine Jocher, Dan Price, Harriet Herring, and John Gillin. Harvey Smith, a masterful teacher, influenced me most of all; to his zeal for sociological analysis and to his patience with an unyielding graduate student I am deeply indebted.

In an age of itinerant academic life it is rare to have a chance for continuous dialogue with another scholar over a period of several years. I enjoyed this luxury twice—with George Tracy in Chapel Hill and with Clyde Wilson in Texas and Missouri. Many of the ideas in the following pages are the direct or indirect result of these dialogues.

A word of thanks, also, to Lillie Fryar, Karen Osborne, Adria Paull, Mary Seland, and Jeanne Wilding for their competent typing and proofreading of the various drafts of this book.

Finally, I should like to thank the editors and publishers of the *Harvard Educational Review* and the *Administrative Science Quarterly* for permission to incorporate material I had previously published in these journals. Also, thanks to the Chandler Publishing Company for permission to quote from Burton Clark's *Educating the Expert Society;* to the editors and publishers of *Human Organization* for permission to quote from Donald F. Roy's " 'Banana Time' . . ."; to the Educational Media Branch, Department of Health, Education, and Welfare and the University of Missouri for permission to use the material in Chapter 1 developed under Contract 2-20-004; and to Justin Huang for permission to include our joint paper as the appendix to this book.

F. E. K.

Contents

.... AUTONOMY and ORGANIZATION

Introduction

. . . the division of labor unites at the same time that it opposes . . .

Emile Durkheim, *The Division of Labor in Society*

Sociologists are sometimes accused of looking at human societies as though they were systems of constraint, social arrangements that control the people within them without permitting them much flexibility.[1] One does not have to look very far to see that in actuality people are not completely subservient to the demands of their society. To be sure, they live up to the rules of their society much of the time. They probably succumb to the expectations of their friends, neighbors, and colleagues most of the time. But they also act independently. Sometimes they violate social rules. Sometimes they defy the raised eyebrows of their friends and neighbors. Such behavior can be called deviance from social constraints. Yet there is also legitimate independence, behavior that is not closely scrutinized, behavior that is *expected* to be different. The scientific researcher is expected to develop new explanations, the creative artist new ways of expressing insights. Such legitimate independence is as much a part of the existing social arrangements as are the rules that specify precisely how people should behave. When one emphasizes the ways in which the society constrains the individual, one is likely to ignore the many and varied ways that the same society also demands independent action. The purpose of this book is to indicate some of the ways in which independent behavior is woven into the fabric of society, to show how independence is actually incorporated into social arrangements.

The underlying theme of these studies is that a degree of independence exists within most social arrangements. Be they large-scale organizations, such as hospitals, schools, or prisons, or small-scale interactions among a few persons, social arrangements contain not only controlled and predictable activities, but also activities that are relatively autonomous. The basic proposition is that autonomy, defined as absence of external constraint, is an ingredient in many, if not all, social arrangements and is incorporated into the very structure of social relationships.

One is inclined to think of autonomy as *separation* from a social context, or as activity that isolates an individual from other persons. In contrast, autonomy is here regarded as a force that binds people together. The assumption is that when there are complicated interactions among people there must be spheres of behavior that are relatively free from surveillance and that such spheres of freedom are necessary in the interest of fruitful interaction.

Two fundamental questions need to be considered. First, if one accepts the premise that autonomy is part of social structures and not merely deviance from them, one must ask what sort of functions autonomy serves within these structures? And second, how is autonomy built into social arrangements; that is, how is autonomy itself structured? Both questions are taken up in each of the following chapters. In the chapter on schools, a general scheme is developed that shows how autonomy may be identified in roles occupied by persons in large social organizations. The following kinds of questions are posed: Does the person who has a work role in an organization have autonomy in his work tasks, and if so, in which aspects of his work? Does he have autonomy outside his work tasks, and if so, can he enact these within the organization in which he works? From the functional viewpoint an attempt is made to show the spheres of behavior where teachers and pupils, respectively, must have autonomy if the school is to achieve its goals. The same role scheme is used in the chapter on blue-collar factory workers. But there the objective is to show that autonomy may not only be necessary for achieving the general goals of an organization, but that it may also be crucial in helping an organization adapt to its environment and achieve an optimal level of internal integration. The argument is made that workers are incompletely integrated into factories, as they do not ordinarily share in the company's profits and do not take part in policy making. But in exchange for this disfranchisement they are permitted considerable autonomy outside their work tasks, though still within the factory. They can bring much of the workingman's style of life into the factory, even though it involves behavior that is alien to the bureaucratic-administrative patterns of behavior. This perspective sets the stage for combining formal and informal practices into a unified theory of organizational structure.[2] Stated differently, this explanation of informal patterns emphasizes that one way for a system to adapt to its environment is to permit the "external" system a limited and controlled degree of participation in the "internal" system.[3]

In Chapter 3 autonomy is studied in relation to power. Sociologists tend to adopt Max Weber's view that power is the likelihood of getting obedience.[4] The view implies that there is some discretion, or autonomy, in the hands of the person doing the obeying. But where does his autonomy lie? How can he exercise it? To develop systematic answers requires a systematic scheme about the nature of power. Amitai Etzioni has developed a scheme about the ways in which control is exercised in complex organizations.[5] This scheme is taken as the point of departure for showing how autonomy exists under different forms of power. For each of Etzioni's types of control there is proposed a type of autonomy that is necessarily part of that form of control. The scheme includes suggestions as to the ways in which autonomy is structured and the functions it serves in the respective ways of controlling people.

Professionals are our society's guardians and dispensers of

specialized knowledge. The social arrangements under which they operate are of great importance. There was a time when professionals operated largely as independent private practitioners. The lawyer had his own office; the physician had his own office. The sociologist studying these professionals had to dwell on the relationship between them and their clients. In modern times, however, professionals are more and more to be found in large, complex organizations. The practice of law is increasingly centered in large law offices; the practice of medicine is increasingly centered in large hospitals. In this situation the professional works alongside other professionals, and all these professionals must, somehow, operate within a common administrative arrangement. In this context the sociologist must try to understand more than the professional's relationship to a client. He must understand the professional's relationships to his professional colleagues and to the administration of the organization in which he operates. He must also understand the history and tradition of the particular professionals in order to ascertain what sort of commitment their members have to a particular body of knowledge and set of skills. All these points underlie the field study of pathologists.

Pathologists are highly specialized physicians. They ordinarily do not have patients of their own and are, therefore, dependent upon other physicians. They are also closely affected by the administrative policies of hospitals since their main facility, the laboratory, often requires financial support from the hospitals. Chapters 5, 6, and 7 offer case studies of how some pathologists actually organize their professional practice. Being case studies, they do not, of course, provide an adequate indication of how all pathologists organize their practice. But each case does provide an illustration of an integrated set of solutions to the profession's major problems. Each case differs in how it resolves the problems (the problems were previously isolated in a survey of the medical literature). Each case displays a different way of balancing areas in which external constraints are accepted against areas in which autonomy is asserted.

The pathology study includes a section on university hospitals. Here one gets a picture of the research-minded academician who is involved both in the active practice of his own profession and in the training of students who will be practitioners. The issues and dilemmas of the pathologists-in-universities doubtless have similarity to problems of other professionals who are members of universities. The pathologist's solutions should be of interest to them.

Assuming that one can state precisely where autonomy exists in particular social arrangements, one still needs to discover *how much* autonomy is necessary. How much autonomy must the physician have from his patient in order to perform his medical tasks? How much autonomy must schools have from parents if they are to do an effective job of teaching? In this book no full-scale assault is made on this problem, but a start is offered: In the Appendix two formal mathematical approaches to autonomy are presented. Hopefully, these approaches will be the beginning of an effort to develop quantitative formulas that state concisely how much autonomy is necessary within particular types of social arrangements.

Finally, a word about systems. By claiming that autonomy is part of the structure of social systems one is saying, in effect, that social systems contain component parts that are relatively indeterminate. This assertion appears to fly in the face of the well-accepted conception of the nature of systems. Surely systems contain precisely interrelated parts. For instance, Talcott Parsons and Edward A. Shils state, "The most general and fundamental property of a system is the interdependence of parts or variables." [6] What must be realized is the fact that for many systems the structural parts need not, indeed cannot, be described very exactly. For instance, social structures are often described in terms of norms. Thus, the role of physician may be described in terms of certain norms that govern his behavior toward patients. He is expected to exclude his own economic self-interest, to adopt objectively verified scientific procedures, and to concern himself specifically with the patient's illness. These criteria do not specify what the physician actually does while he has dealings with patients. They merely specify the limits within which his behavior must fall if it is to remain acceptable within our conception of how a physician should behave toward patients. What the physician actually does in particular situations is left indeterminate by the norms, except that he must not transgress the limits set by the norms. In short, the limits can be stated very clearly and precisely, but there is still a sphere where behavior is left indeterminate. However, the indeterminance within the limits is not an unfortunate failure of the system. On the contrary, it is a necessity that enables the physician to have the flexibility to adapt to the conditions he meets in the concrete situation in which he actually finds himself.

The idea of partial indeterminance of systems is foreshadowed in Ludwig von Bertalanffy's writings on open systems, especially on biological systems.[7] Bertalanffy says these systems have a "continuous inflow and outflow, building up and breaking down of the component material of the system."[8] He stresses the interdependence between different systems. For instance,

> . . . a living organism is an object maintaining itself in an orderly flow of events wherein the higher systems appear persistent in the exchange of the subordinate ones . . .[9]

and

> . . . what appears to be persistent at one level is in fact maintained in a continuous change, formation, growth, wearing out, and death of systems of the next lower level: of chemical components in the cell, of cells in a multicellular organism, and of individuals in a [species] . . .[10]

In this picture—Bertalanffy calls it the steady state—systems benefit from a degree of openness toward other systems. The steady state implies that even the subordinate systems have some degree of stability; they are not destroyed by the superior system despite the fact that some of their components are continually being destroyed. The present book suggests that one variant of open systems is systems that have a degree of internal flexibility. That is, some of the structures within the system have a degree of indeterminance, and this, too, can have significance for the system.

Now let us turn to a sociological consideration of indeterminance in systems by looking at autonomy within complex social organizations. Complex organizations—such as factories, hospitals, and prisons—are chosen because a sizable amount of sociological research has been done on these structures.[11] Many writers believe that within these "bureaucratic" organizations there exists an enormous amount of depersonalization and alienation.[12] Undoubtedly most prisoners resent being in prison; undoubtedly many factory workers do work that is dull and stupefying. The seeds for discontent surely exist. But before assuming a picture of massive disorganization one must realize that one's own orientations may be coloring these findings; facts do *not* speak for themselves. Among present-day sociologists two major competing orientations are those of the structuralists (or structure-functionalists) and those of the conflictists. This book attempts to create a bridge between them.[13] Returning to alienation, among structuralists the existence of alienation, or opposition of any sort, is difficult to handle; indeed, C. Wright Mills suggested that structuralists tend to ignore it.[14] On the other hand, for theorists who emphasize that conflict is the most fundamental social process, alienation is apt to be exaggerated and lead to the assumption that there is no order except that which rests on suppression of alienated people. The present book is written from a structural point of view. But it tries to wrestle with the very issues that the conflict theorists have emphasized: the need for independence within social relationships and the persistence of divergent interests and objectives among people who must, somehow, deal with one another. It tries to show that there are ways whereby independence and divergence are incorporated into stable social structures without destroying the system and without loss of potency for the subordinate units.

NOTES ...

1. Dennis Wrong, "The Over-socialized Conception of Man in Modern Sociology," *Psychoanalysis and the Psychoanalytic Review*, XLIX, 2 (1962), 52–69.

2. Many scholars have shown that informal patterns play an important part in social structures. For instance, Charles H. Page has shown that one of the functions of informal patterns is to circumvent formal patterns. See his "Bureaucracy's Other Face," *Social Forces*, 25 (1946), 88–94. In this book, especially in Chapter 2, an attempt is made to show that one structural model of organizations can incorporate both "formal" and "informal" patterns.

Previous writings, such as those of Page, have recognized that members of bureaucracies tend to carve out some autonomy for themselves. The present study attempts to incorporate this into the formal model.

3. The distinction between internal and external systems has been developed most cogently by George C. Homans. See his *The Human Group* (New York: Harcourt, Brace, 1950).

4. Max Weber, *The Theory of Social and Economic Organization*, A. M. Henderson and Talcott Parsons, tr. (New York: Free Press, 1947), p. 324.

5. Amitai Etzioni, *A Comparative Analysis of Complex Organizations* (New York: Free Press, 1961).

6. Talcott Parsons and Edward A. Shils, eds., *Toward a General Theory of Action* (New York: Harper, 1962), p. 107.

7. Ludwig von Bertalanffy, *Problems of Life* (New York: Harper, 1960)

8. *Ibid.*, p. 125.

9. *Ibid.*, pp. 134–135.

10. *Ibid.*, p. 124.

11. The reader who wishes to see autonomy considered in a larger, society-wide context might consult the work of S. N. Eisenstadt. See especially his "Transformation of Social, Political, and Cultural Orders in Modernization," *American Sociological Review*, 30, 5 (1965), 659–673, and *The Systems of Empires* (New York: Free Press, 1963).

12. See, for example, Erving Goffman, *Asylums* (Chicago: Aldine, 1961). In relation to workers in factories, Chris Argyris writes, "the needs of healthy individuals are not congruent with the requirements of formal organization." See Argyris, *Understanding Organizational Behavior* (Homewood, Ill.: Dorsey Press, 1960), p. 14.

13. Gerhard Lenski also tries to bridge this gap. However, he leans toward the conflict school, whereas the present book leans toward the structuralist school. See Lenski's *Power and Privilege* (New York: McGraw-Hill, 1966).

14. C. Wright Mills, *The Sociological Imagination* (New York: Grove Press, 1961), p. 23.

part i ANALYTIC STUDIES OF AUTONOMY

1

The Identification of Autonomy

in Complex Organizations:

The School

The school is a complex social organization. It is complex because
it includes many different persons in interaction who perform
many different functions. It is a social organization because the
participants are interdependent and their actions socially promulgated and enforced. The study of complex organizations is cur-
rently receiving much attention by sociologists, political scientists,
and others concerned with the study of large-scale administration
of human effort. Various formulations that have emerged from
these studies can be applied to the analysis of schools. Schools
share organizational characteristics with factories, social work
agencies, and military units; but they also have unique aspects.
Yet even consideration of the uniqueness of the school will add
to knowledge not only of schools but also of complex organizations, provided that the consideration proceeds in a sufficiently
analytic manner.

The use both of the literature of educational research and the literature of complex organizations will be selective. The goal is not to integrate these writings, as Neal Gross, W. W. Charters, Jr., R. J. Havighurst, and B. L. Neugarten have already done for educational studies and Peter M. Blau, W. R. Scott, and Amitai Etzioni have done for complex-organization studies,[1] but to develop a more powerful model of complex organizations so that they can be understood more adequately.

Specifically, a model of the school is developed that focused on diversification as a central principle. It is postulated that diversification is reflected in the social structure of schools, especially in the existence of patterns of autonomy incorporated into the very structure of schools. Autonomy is defined here as behavior that is not controlled by an external agency. Teachers ordinarily have autonomy—that is, independence from external control—in their classroom conduct, although the amount and scope of their autonomy varies in different schools. Whatever the scope, it is proposed that *some* autonomy is accorded the teacher and that this autonomy is recognized and incorporated into the operating codes of the school. Giving a teacher the right to decide how many tests to give and how to seat children in his classroom exemplifies a way in which autonomy is structured. In other words, the rules that provide for a sphere of autonomy for the teacher are postulated to be as much a part of the official rules of the school as are the rules that stipulate a sphere of compliance for the teacher; both are part of the structure of the school. It is further suggested that there are spheres of autonomy for all participants in schools, for children as well as adults.

Using the sources of diversity as a starting point, spheres of autonomy will be outlined. Then, adopting a typology of autonomy structure in relation to social positions and roles, postulations are made concerning the form in which autonomy tends to be structured within the social organization of the school. Although primary consideration is given to the internal structure of schools, external pressures are not ignored as sources of autonomy for school participants and as potential encroachments upon the autonomy of the school as a whole.

Other sociological writings on complex organizations also

dwell on the organization's adaptation to a variety of pressures.[2] But these writings tend to view organizations primarily as amalgamation processes in which competing interests and pressures are reduced to the extent that the organization can pursue a course toward relatively specific goals. In contrast, the present study of schools views diversity as a persistent element within organizations that tends to be incorporated into their very structure without being reduced to insignificant proportions. Diversity is thereby harnessed by the organization in the process of accomplishing its missions.

The present model also differs from existing conceptions of authority that view authority as applying uniformly to all segments within an organization. All activities are governed by authority; actions that depart from the established, all-pervasive authority are considered to be actual or potential forms of deviance. The diversification model, on the other hand, points to limitations of authority in all segments of any organization. Each segment— each division, each department, each occupant of a position— has a sphere of action that is only minimally controlled by the whole organization (in addition to a sphere that is very definitely controlled by the organization's authority structure). An attempt will be made to improve the analysis of social processes involving schools by proposing a change in perspective that suggests that certain specifiable spheres of autonomy for the school's members are necessary if the school is to accomplish its missions.

The validity of the present perspective can be ascertained only when the propositions and questions it raises are subjected to empirical test. The example of the school raises questions, explicitly and implicitly, rather than answering them. Thus, although the specific spheres in which teachers and pupils need autonomy are indicated, there is no attempt to determine optimal levels of autonomy; that is, how much autonomy makes for sufficient flexibility without, at the same time, threatening the integration of the school. The last section attempts to relate the autonomy theory to specific educational problems. It offers no startling new answers, but it suggests some reformulations of issues. For example, it proposes, but does not empirically test, that the "adolescent subculture" theme may exaggerate the existence of conflict between youths and adults by assuming that divergence necessarily implies conflict.

Sociological Approaches to the Study of Complex Organizations

Sociological writings on complex organizations invariably refer to Max Weber. Weber's historical and analytical studies of bureaucracy have provided the core formulations regarding the social structure of complex organizations that sociologists use to this day. According to Weber, bureaucracy is a rational organization of human effort; its members are chosen on the basis of ability to perform specific tasks, and responsibility for accomplishing these tasks is incorporated into established positions, each of which is systematically related to other positions (usually in a hierarchical arrangement). Responsibilities and duties are built into positions through a system of rules that specify the contribution of each position to the whole organization. The mission of the organization, for example, the production of certain goods at a profit to the owner, underlies the entire system and provides the raison d'être for all the rules. It was Weber's belief that bureaucracy is the most efficient and rational form of harnessing human energy that has yet been devised, paralleling the harnessing of physical energy by machines. Weber's work has given rise to a flourishing sociological specialization, the study of complex organizations.

It is probably fair to say that recent sociological theories of complex organizations are a series of footnotes to Weber.[3] That this is so creates an ironic situation, since virtually all empirical studies of complex organizations have pointed to inadequacies in the Weberian model. Studies of complex organizations have consistently discovered informal activities—activities that are not included in the formal set of organizational rules of prescribed behavior—which constitute anomalies in the Weberian model.

The early industrial studies by Mayo and his colleagues leave no doubt that informal behavior is often patterned and socially organized and is not merely idiosyncratic individual deviation.[4] More recent studies, for instance those done by Blau, have demonstrated that such patterns of informal activity are often functionally necessary for the organization's members to accomplish their part of the organization's mission and, therefore, are related to formal structure.[5] On the other hand, many studies have found that informal activity may actually systematically curtail these goals. The best-known example of this effect is control of production by workers.

There is, as yet, no completely adequate formulation that links informal patterns to a comprehensive theory of complex organizations. For example, Talcott Parsons reflects the Weberian model when he identifies the defining characteristic of complex organizations as the "primacy of orientation to the attainment of a specific goal." [6] The dominant theme in Parsons' conception is a "decision-making process, which controls the utilization of the resources of the system as a whole in the interest of the goal, and the processes by which those responsible for such decisions can count on the mobilization of these resources in the interest of the goal." [7] There is little place in this scheme for patterned informal behavior. It is, at best, deviant behavior. This state of affairs prevails in spite of Blau's demonstration of the existence of system-supporting patterns.

Blau and Scott state that the distinguishing feature of formal organizations is that they are "deliberately established for a certain purpose"; that they "have not spontaneously emerged in the course of social interaction but have been consciously designed *a priori* to anticipate and guide interaction and activities." [8] The statement is probably an accurate declaration about formal organization. But, as in the formulation by Parsons, there is overwhelming emphasis on a single goal and on rational organization to achieve the goal. Informal patterns are essentially peripheral categories. This will be discussed more fully in Chapter 2, where an attempt is made to integrate "formal" and "informal" patterns into one theory.

Theorists have tried to accommodate informal behavior by proposing that informal and formal structures coexist within organizations. Formal structures are made up of the Weberian scheme of positions in rational relation to organizational goals; informal structures are regarded as occurring inevitably as organizations adapt to their setting. The formal and informal structures are often viewed as organically fused "natural systems" where an equilibrium process develops among the component parts.[9] Alvin W. Gouldner has suggested that this model tends to "lose sight of the autonomy of the system parts, of their autonomy strivings and strategies, as well as of the ways in which such strategies may induce tensions among the other segments or within the system as a whole." [10] Gouldner believes that autonomy patterns should be incorporated into the social-system model of complex organizations. This view can be taken a step further with the postulation that *autonomy patterns are distinctly structured within complex organizations* and can be the subject of orderly conceptual and empirical assessment. It will also be argued that some forms of autonomy are functionally necessary and therefore cannot be regarded as merely deviant action.

Autonomy Structures in Complex Organization

"Autonomous," according to Webster, refers to a state that is "self-governing . . . without outside control." [11] Similarly, in this book "autonomous" refers to the independence of subunits of an organization from control by other parts of the organization or even by the whole organization. For some purposes the entire organization may be regarded as an autonomous unit. The nearest parallel usage of "autonomous" can be found in biology where, according to Webster, it is a state "existing independently; responding or reacting independently of the whole." [12] In the present context, the "whole" is usually a complex organization, such as a school, a factory, a hospital, or a prison, but it can also be a community or a society. Only those types of autonomous actions that can be related to the social structure of complex organizations are of concern here. Consideration of purely personal autonomy patterns are thus excluded. It is postulated that patterned forms of autonomy exist within complex organizations that, by definition, exhibit independence from external control but, nonetheless, are part of the organizational structure.

Two functional bases for autonomy structure are investigated: *autonomy structure related to specialization* and *autonomy structure related to the affiliations of members of the organization.* The nature of the objectives in the first (including the tasks to be performed and the characteristics of the objects that are being processed) produces requirements for autonomy to enable the accomplishment of these tasks. These requirements touch the individual functionary. In order to exercise his specialized judgment, he must be protected from his own superiors, his "clients," and his fellow specialists. Included in the second are affiliations *outside* the "host" organization and affiliational variability *inside* the "host" organization. The emphasis in the discussion of both bases will be on the manner in which autonomy is socially structured in relation to positions located in the organization. Position and role are used here in the traditional sociological sense: position is a place in a set of social relationships; role is the behavior expected of the occupant of a position. It is assumed that autonomy is not an all-or-nothing entity. The scheme uses types of role specifications in relation to positions, as follows:

Forms of Autonomy: How Autonomy Is Specified for Positions

First, autonomy is internal to organizational roles and is (1) enacted *in the* organization and/or (2) enacted *outside* the organization. Second, autonomy is external to organizational roles and is (1) enacted *in* the organization and/or (2) enacted *outside* the organization.

Autonomy that is "internal" to one's organizational role refers to a sphere of autonomy regarded as an intrinsic part of the role occupant's contribution to the organization. Autonomy that is "external" to one's organizational role refers to a sphere of autonomy regarded as extraneous to one's organizational contribution. The school superintendent thus has duties in the area of policy formulation. He also has a degree of autonomy in this sphere that is regarded as a legitimate part of his role in the school system (internal autonomy). This autonomy is exercised *in* the organization, in the course of his day-to-day work. But the superintendent's role is usually so defined that even when he leaves the school buildings he remains the school representative. When he plays golf at the country club, when he takes part in a charity campaign in the community, when he sits on the local hospital board of trustees, he remains in the role (his "master role") of school superintendent and continues to enact this organizational role, in both the compliant and the autonomous features. The superintendent's role is broadly defined in a special sense. Within the school system he has a broad sphere of autonomy as part of his official role. Outside the school system his autonomy is also substantial, but it is limited by his organizational membership; he remains *in* the school system even when he goes to the country club. His autonomy external to the organizational role is narrow.[13]

Autonomy Structures Based on Specialization

Specialization of Tasks   It has been suggested that "the existence of [complex] organization . . . is a consequence of the division of labor in society." [14] That is, modern societies require considerable specialization in the labor that individuals perform, and complex organizations serve to coordinate the efforts of such specialists. But if the division of labor has fostered the development of complex organizations, it has also left its mark on the internal structure of these organizations. The organization must permit the specialists to deploy their specialized skills. When the skills are relatively simple, such as the ability to tighten a bolt on an automobile frame that moves along a conveyor belt, the formal instructions can specify precisely the work that is to be done. When the skills are highly complex, such as the physician's task of diagnosing illness, the formal rules of procedure cannot be full and detailed; indeed, they must explicitly permit a considerable degree of autonomous judgment on the part of the physician, including the right to be wrong. Similar rights to professional autonomy are encountered in universities. These claims to autonomy are essential ingredients in the utilization of highly specialized knowledge.

The claims present dilemmas for the administrators of organizations. These administrators are not able to exercise close control over specialists since they do not have the same technical training, but they still have responsibility for coordinating the work of the specialists. As a result, there exists a sizable literature on conflicts between specialists seeking independence and administrators seeking dependable and calculable performance (e.g., academic freedom from arbitrary control by boards of education). It is a conflict between the "substantive expert" and the "administrative expert." [15] As Gouldner has pointed out, Weber's formulation contains the assumption that all runs smoothly in the bureaucracy, despite the inherent dilemma involved in the fact that "on the one side it [is] administration based on expertise, while on the other it [is] administration based on discipline." [16] It is suggested here that restraints placed upon the expert must inevitably be balanced against a degree of autonomy. The proposition that follows from recognition of this balance is that *the greater the degree of specialized knowledge and skills required of the occupant of a position, the greater the degree of autonomy that accrues to the position;* or, the greater the degree of specialized knowledge and skills required of the incumbent of a position, the less discipline can be exerted over the position by the administration of the organization. But it is important to note that the reference is to a role for which autonomy is internal to organizational membership; the proposition would not hold for a role where autonomy is external to organizational membership (see page 32). Paul C. Rosenblatt has suggested a related proposition based on working contacts with others: the less assistance available (from peers, for example), the greater the autonomy that accrues to a position.[17]

There is an additional facet to the specialist-administrator situation. The administrator may also be regarded as a specialist, whose "specialized" task is the coordination of effort within the organization. Coordination is a sphere of responsibility that can readily encroach upon the autonomy of technical specialists. In the school, for example, administrative responsibility includes the coordination of teaching by different instructors so that transfer of students and movement of pupils from grade to grade are accompanied by a minimal amount of frustration to the children and disruption to the school. This coordination requires restrictions upon the autonomy of the individual teachers. The coordination of activity, which is the necessary task of the administrative specialists, thus limits the performance by the other specialists. Yet, as Chester I. Barnard has pointed out, administrative activity depends heavily upon the willing participation of subordinates.[18]

The school's most numerous specialists are the teachers. They operate under an administrative regime of nonspecialists, the school board, which sets administrative policies. The board delegates authority to persons with specific educational training to instruct; the size of the schools and number of their administrative echelons vary with the size and social character of the community. In the lower echelons, where teaching is performed, the lowest degree of administrative power is enjoyed (in terms of the ability to influence the total organization), and the greatest technical specialization exists. Yet specialization requires autonomy. How is teacher autonomy achieved? Doubtless there are many tactics and strategies by which teachers achieve a degree of autonomy. But data, in the form of objective studies, are not available. It would be interesting, for example, to see whether the teacher with a strong personal following among pupils can assert more independence in his relationships with the school administration than the teacher without such a following.

In addition to autonomy patterns affecting the relationships between specialists and administrative staffs of schools, there are problems of autonomy arising from relationships among different specialists. Rivalries between academics and athletics, between "fundamental" and "practical" fields, have long been recognized. These venerable enmities now seem to be joined by new protagonists: the itinerant specialist versus the local, established teacher. The former goes from school to school helping to set up new programs—remedial reading, new mathematics, and so forth. The latter is involved in day-to-day teaching of specific subjects to specific groups of children. Each specialist has a different functional assignment. The itinerant specialist is attuned to discovering weaknesses in the existing programs, introducing improved procedures, and instituting wholly new approaches; the established teacher (and the administrative staff) is geared to minimizing disruptions, continuing existing programs, and generally preserving the orderly flow of activity in order to produce a fairly predictable product—the pupil who can pass on to the next grade, the pupil who can gain admission to college, the pupil who can get a job. The teacher's reluctance to change existing programs is understandable, for he will be called upon to carry out the new programs and, if things go wrong, to pick up the pieces. At the same time, to do his job, the itinerant specialist requires the collaboration of the teacher, possibly the same teacher whose job he is sharply modifying.

In an overall sense the functions of these two specialists are, of course, complementary. But in day-to-day operations their activities may be antithetical, and they may require protection from each other if each is to have enough independence and flexibility to fulfill his functional mission. Whereas the established teacher must be protected from the disruptive effects of new programs, some of which may not work out well, the itinerant specialist must be protected from insistence by school staffs on immediate and complete success of new programs if he is to innovate and discover new methods of teaching and motivating students. More broadly, specialization among members of complex organizations implies not only that different functions are being pursued within the organization, but also that the accomplishment of each of these functions requires some autonomy. Formulated as a proposition, *accomplishment of functional contributions to a system requires a degree of autonomy from that system.*

Specialists tend to be organized into departments. Their quests for autonomy, therefore, tend to involve interdepartmental relationships. It follows that when quests for autonomy involve interaction between departments that are within the same echelon —that is, where neither department is clearly superordinate to the other—the organization must then provide protection for the autonomy of each department. Otherwise the departments will themselves establish ways of protecting their functionally necessary autonomy. Such devices as reservation of time periods for particular subjects and separation of classes into rooms are ways of protecting teachers and their pupils from encroachments and, thereby, constitute protection for a degree of autonomy.

When functional specialization involves departments or other units that are on different levels in a hierarchy, the difference in power can be relied upon to protect the higher from encroachments by the lower unit (sheer power need rarely be invoked when it is known to exist). But safeguarding autonomy of subordinates from superordinates calls for social inventiveness that must often be sub rosa; methods must be used that do not involve open confrontation with the superior. The literature and folklore on bureaucracy are replete with examples of such efforts. Robert K. Merton's "retreatism," where the individual prevents access to himself, is probably a favorite device.[19] Referring to civil servants, S. M. Lipset writes about the functional need for officials to protect themselves from their superiors:

> A department official is not only interested in whether a minister's proposals can be effectively put into operation, but must also be concerned with the effect of such policies on the traditional policies of the department, and long term relations of the department with other groups in the government and in the community . . . A reform which may be socially desirable, but which disrupts the continuity of practices and interpersonal relations within the department, will often be resisted by a top ranking civil servant. He is obliged to protect those beneath him in the administrative hierarchy from the negative consequences of a change in policy.[20]

Little empirical study has been made of autonomy patterns among organizational elites, since most studies of informal behavior deal with persons in low echelons.[21] Remarks about the elite in this connection are, therefore, largely speculative. It would seem that work obligations are usually stipulated in less detail at the higher level than they are at lower levels. At high levels the very prescriptions regarding expected behavior leave greater scope for autonomy within the formally structured role than they do at lower levels. Autonomy at the top is not as readily defined as deviant behavior as is autonomy in the lower ranks. It is therefore less visible to researchers. This suggests that *autonomy may be clearest by contrast, when rules for compliance are most clearly stated.* The high degree of autonomy at top levels requires personnel to set their own limits to a far greater extent than do those at low levels. For the latter, the organization sets more limits, such as work hours, place of work, and pace for performing work.

There is a limit to the amount of autonomy that can prevail if the organization is to continue to function. A clear example is the progressive-education movement, which was presumably intended to maximize the autonomy potential of the child. Among the dilemmas that emerged, and that are relevant to our topic, were the questions: How much autonomy? and: When does autonomy degenerate into utter intractability or revolt? Probably the debate over the optimum degree of autonomy for the child is often resolved, not on the basis of ideological preferences or the needs of the child, but on the basis of the limited tolerance for autonomy within the organization in which the child exists (family, schools, community). This setting of limits to autonomy can also be regarded as the control of entropy by these systems; there are boundaries to the amount of disorder they can stand.

In addition to features that permit autonomy within organizations, whole organizations inevitably have a degree of autonomy from the rest of society. If this fact seems too obvious for amplification, the reader is reminded of the current emphasis on the "impact of society" on the family, on schools, on businesses, and so forth. Yet, such organized units as the family enjoy sizable guarantees of autonomy.[22] There is protection against intruders—the physical intruder into the family's homestead as well as the affectional intruder into intrafamilial ties ("alienation of affection"). The autonomy is guaranteed by law and custom.

Autonomy patterns of the school as an entity are particularly important, but they have not been studied adequately. The lack of autonomy through the impact of society on schools is illustrated by studies showing the influences of pervasive middle-class values on teacher behavior and the impact of community power structure and social-class patterns on the operation of schools.[23] According to these studies, schools are but pawns in the hands of community forces. They are at the mercy of school boards made up of business and social leaders of the community; they are harassed by middle-class-dominated PTA's; and they are infiltrated by teachers and administrators who have been brain-washed by their own training and their own aspirations to move into middle-class society. Although these views have been challenged,[24] there appears to be no significant research showing the tactics and strategies used by schools to preserve a degree of autonomy. Undoubtedly schools have ways of protecting themselves from external interference, at least to some extent. It would be instructive to find out how this is done. Which strategies are successful and which are not? What price is paid for a degree of autonomy from external control?

Specialization of Objects Being Processed   It is a premise of this study that the characteristics of the object being processed will introduce requirements of autonomy, both for the organization that is its processing agency and for the object itself. In the case of the school, the objects being processed are human beings. The child's active learning and socialization is promoted in the school, but this process has begun before the child reaches the school and will continue after he finishes school. And even during the years the child is in school there will be learning and socialization influences upon him other than those of the school. For the school this diversity of influences means functional interdependence with these other agencies of education and socialization—with families, peer groups, organizations of higher education, and occupational organizations. The school must, somehow, provide continuity with early family training, demonstrate that its efforts have usefulness for higher education and adult occupational requirements and fit in with the child's contemporary world. It is our hypothesis that if the school is to perform its specialized function, there must be a degree of autonomy from these other agencies; the "conjunction" with these agencies must be balanced by a degree of "disjunction." To clarify this hypothesis, let us consider the specialized function of the school that calls for autonomy from the child's family and community.

A most important feature of the school's function is that it introduces the child to cosmopolitan concepts that wean him away from his local context and attune him to a larger context. The child is not taught to add up the family bills, he is taught to add; he is not taught to read the family's mementos, he is taught to read. Even where local participation is encouraged by the school, it is apt to be done in the name of a larger perspective: One should participate in elections because elections are important to the preservation of the existing political system, not just because candidate Jones promises more roads for the county than does candidate Smith. Since cosmopolitanism is, by definition, at odds with localism, the school requires a degree of autonomy from local pressures if it is to accomplish this task of generalizing and broadening the child's knowledge and social participation.

In addition to pressures from external sources, schools are

subject to internal threat from their objects; this also creates requirements for autonomy. Since the objects are humans, there will necessarily be social relationships between the objects and the members of the processing agency. These social relationships may encroach upon the school's mission. The permanent student, the overly affectionate student, the overly alienated student all represent threats to the school's mission because they interfere with the teaching process. Schools, like other organizations that have human objects, often preserve their mission by establishing a degree of autonomy for the organization through distinctive role definitions. Differentiation is made between the transients and the permanent members of the organization—between pupils and teachers of the school, just as between customer and clerk of the retail store and between client and bureaucrat of the employment agency. Transients are discouraged from permanent affiliation with the organization, and persons occupying permanent positions are encouraged to act dispassionately and to curtail the individualizing of transients. Just as the store clerk is expected to treat all customers courteously and not to grant favors to one customer that he would not be able to grant to other customers, teachers are expected to show no preference or personal liking for a particular pupil while neglecting other pupils. The dispassionate attitude helps to render the service at the same time that it prevents the transient's personalized involvement with functionaries of the organization. But, within the prescribed limits of dispassionate behavior the teacher is permitted considerable independence. The teacher may sit or stand while he leads his class; he may read children's grades aloud or tell each child his grade separately. As long as his behavior toward the pupils is not individualizing, he is at liberty to be independent. This autonomy that the organization exercises vis-à-vis its human objects is a functional necessity.

Because children are the objects being processed by schools, they too are in a special relationship that requires that a degree of autonomy be explicitly safeguarded for them. Children are clients who benefit from professional services; that is, there are presumed to be areas in which their interests are best served by professionals.[25] In this respect, children are in the same position as medical or legal clients. The relationship between professional and client is essentially asymmetrical: the client comes to the professional for help; the professional has superior knowledge in the area of the client's problems; the client is a poor judge of his own needs. In the well-established professions the autonomy of the client is safeguarded by rules that govern the behavior of the professional. As Parsons has indicated, the professional is expected to be fair, disinterested, and rational in his approach to the client.[26] It may be hypothesized that *without some organized protection of the client's autonomy neither the role of professional nor that of the client would be acceptable or permanent.* A related hypothesis is that *if an asymmetrical relationship is to persist under noncoercive conditions, a degree of autonomy must be guaranteed for the person in the weaker role.* The assumption is that guarantees of autonomy for the weaker role give permanence to the relationship by supplying rules that remove temptation from the professional and foster the rational deployment of his skills. It is of interest that even though the teacher role lacks some of the prestige of other professions, it does, nonetheless, incorporate the guarantees of autonomy for the client, the child.

In addition to being a client, the fact that the child is regarded as a legal minor potentially adds to his disadvantages in the relationship. But here, also, there are structural guarantees for the child's autonomy. Teachers, and other school personnel, are regarded as quasi-guardians of the child, at least during school hours. Also, the child's other guardians—usually his parents—have access to the school in various ways for the purpose of protecting their child's interests.

Autonomy Structures Based on Affiliations

It has already been suggested that the division of labor in modern society gives rise to technical specialization that, in turn, necessitates functional autonomy patterns in complex organizations. Another result of the division of labor is that individuals are involved in multiple relationships and commitments; people are, simultaneously, members of many social organizations. An important corollary is that individuals do not necessarily have a major commitment to each relationship in which they are involved. For example, a study of career choices indicated that persons may adopt an occupation without having made a subjective commitment to that occupation.[27] Similarly, members of a complex organization may have very limited allegiance to that organization.

Crosscutting Affiliation Most complex organizations must adapt to the fact that their functionaries have active group affiliations beyond the confines of the organization. (There are exceptions, such as monasteries, where outside affiliations are permanently severed and prisons, where outside affiliations are at least temporarily severed.) Some of these affiliations, such as family and community ties, do not necessarily affect the organization. But there are others, such as union membership of workers and membership in professional associations by specialists, where the outside loyalty may rival the commitment to the organization in which the individual works. Such affiliations may exist within an organization and yet possess a degree of autonomy from the host organization. Thus fraternities and sororities in colleges and high schools are sometimes regarded as alien to the host organization. J. S. Coleman has suggested that the adolescent subculture constitutes a "distinct community" within the high school.[28] From studies of the extent of the affiliation of professionals with their host organization has emerged the typology of "cosmopolitans" and "locals." [29] "Cosmopolitans" are primarily committed to affiliations beyond the host organization in which they work; "locals" are primarily committed to the host organization. The specialist —the school's vocational counselor, dietitian, or itinerant specialist in accelerated mathematics—has a limited sphere of autonomy in his organizational position but may have considerable autonomy strictly within his specialty. His peer connections, especially if he is a member of a well-developed profession, can assure him of a considerable sphere of autonomy that is external to his organizational role but is enacted in the organization as well as outside it. For example, the vocational counselor who has an independent professional reputation through publications in learned journals or an executive position in a learned society may be permitted considerable opportunity to pursue his own research interests and will be allowed time off to attend professional meetings. The term "cosmopolitan" tends to obscure the fact that the professional who is labeled in this way may be strongly integrated in an organized collectivity of his professional peers. This collectivity crosscuts the boundaries of the local organization and is therefore not always tangible and tractable to other members of the local work setting.

It is important to realize that most complex organizations are not self-sufficient communities. Because complex organizations are specialized structures that serve particular functions, they must be interlocked with other structures. Schools as organizations, for example, exist to prepare children for active participation in adult activities and must therefore allow them a degree of independent activity. Yet by permitting students a degree of autonomy, the school risks the possible hostility to the school's goals by the cliques, clubs, and activities that the students organize. Similarly, schools require teachers who are competent to teach and stimulate students. But teachers' technical competence requires contact with other teachers and schools of education in order to keep up with advances within their fields. Such contact may give rise to a heightened concern with professionalism, such as the desire to elevate the status of teachers and to be permitted to innovate new teaching methods. These, too, can become a threat to schools because they are liable to emphasize a teacher's autonomy over a teacher's compliance with existing school constraints.

The school is committed to permitting members to maintain affiliations that are potentially dangerous to it. Each affiliation involves a degree of autonomy for organization members, yet schools cannot cut off these outside affiliations because the life-lines of their own interdependence with other structures would, thereby, be severed. Hence the school does not have monolithic autonomy; instead, it permits degrees of autonomy for its component subunits. The organization model demonstrating this autonomy would be characterized by divergent allegiances among member units rather than by a unitary system that is centrally controlled.

Affiliational Variability to the Host Organization How much diversion from goals is permitted? Let us reiterate that a specific goal is often thought to be the basic characteristic of an organization.[30] The concern here is *not* with behavior that deviates from organizational rules and goals and is regarded as unacceptable behavior. The concern is with *patterned* behavior that *departs* from prescribed behavior and is regarded as *acceptable* to the organization.

First, it has long been recognized that compliance with a role is rarely absolute and is not expected to be; a degree of leeway is permitted to most role incumbents. This leeway is most operative when the actor can demonstrate strong involvement in an approved goal. When the janitor orders the company president out of his office in order to prim the office for an important visitor, the janitor is clearly overstepping the bounds of his position, but he is proclaiming his concern for the company's impression on the VIP. Longtime employees are occasionally permitted similar types of leeway. They are often regarded as the very embodiment of the organization's traditions and, on this basis, are permitted idiosyncrasies and deviations from expected behavior for which a more recent employee would be punished (e.g., a worker coming to work late, a professor forgetting to meet classes). It can be stated that *an actor's strong commitment to an organization and its goals tends to be accompanied by autonomy privileges.* The commitment, however, is *attributed* to the actor; he may not actually have such a commitment. Usually such commitment is taken for granted for holders of elite positions— executives and persons in leadership positions at every level—and these persons usually enjoy greater autonomy than those under them in the hierarchy. This is presumably based on functional requirements for flexibility among policy makers. Persons at low levels, such as janitors, can occasionally enjoy autonomy privileges, but such persons must explicitly demonstrate their commitment. Their loyalty to the organization and its goals is not as readily taken for granted as is that of the elite. Here a distinction is made between *ascribed* and *achieved* autonomy. In the high echelon, autonomy is ascribed to the position itself and does not have to be achieved by the incumbent.

Summary

The perspective on schools suggested here deliberately focuses on diversification. Diversification brings to mind the popular journalistic picture of amorphousness, which portrays modern society in terms of diverse reference groups and values, or lack of any integrating mechanisms and common ground of any sort. The seeming lack of order is frightening when viewed from the point of view of the human plight, but at the same time it presents an alluring challenge to the researcher because it beckons for the discovery of order amid the chaos. The work of Emile Durkheim contains the rudiment for a scheme that treats diversification as a central phenomenon.[31] Durkheim conceived of modern societies as characterized by high degrees of specialization—division of labor—that require a close organic interdependence of parts. This conception can serve as a starting point for a model of the complex organization that focuses on the divergencies in social organizations.

It has already been claimed that there are various functional requirements that necessitate autonomy within organizations as well as by organizations *in toto*. These autonomy patterns can be conceived structurally as parts of positions. Thus, the school superintendent position includes high internal and low external autonomy. By contrast, low-ranking, unspecialized personnel will have fairly limited amounts of autonomy internal to their organizational position but broad autonomy external to their organizational position. The two types of autonomy are not necessarily mutually exclusive unless one assumes that there is an absolute limit to combined external and internal autonomy; this assumption seems premature. The above hypothetical profiles are summarized in Table 1.

The table reflects that specialists' autonomy tends to be extensive in a narrowly defined sphere. Also, specialists' autonomy depends on the extent of professionalization in their fields. Concerning pupils, we have noted the normative safeguards for them, but they are nonetheless in a weak position vis-à-vis the teacher. Items about pupils and teachers will obviously vary in different types of schools. In small communities the child's external status,

Table 1. Hypothetical Profiles

POSITION	INTERNAL AUTONOMY		EXTERNAL AUTONOMY	
	Within the Organization	*Outside the Organization*	*Within the Organization*	*Outside the Organization*
Superintendent	extensive	extensive	limited	limited
Specialist	medium	limited	extensive	extensive
Pupil (vis-à-vis teacher)	limited	limited	medium	extensive
Teacher (vis-à-vis pupil)	extensive	limited	limited	extensive

especially his family background, traditionally has considerably influenced his school status (which would justify an "extensive" autonomy classification). But recent increases in school size and routinizations de-emphasize the child's external status. Studies of youth culture indicate that the impact of children's nonschool activities intrude into the school. The categorization of the extent of this intrusion as "medium" is frankly a tentative judgment, based on a somewhat intuitive assessment of the existing studies.

Autonomy and Education in the Expert Society

Americans have great faith in education. Yet there is great dissatisfaction with the existing educational machinery, and schools are caught in the resulting turmoil. The traditional functions of education—the perpetuation of the social heritage and the teaching of basic skills to the young—are still recognized as necessary. There is increasing awareness, however, that education is the primary tool for enabling man to participate in the modern world and that educational procedures and content should be geared to this challenge. Modern societies increasingly require technical experts; the educational system is expected to produce these experts. At a time when new fields of technology continue to proliferate, it is difficult for social establishments to produce the needed new experts. The wheels of the existing social establishments grind slowly and their staffs are themselves inadequately trained in the new technologies. A major feature of the technological world is the fact that it is changing at an accelerating pace. New experts are in demand, and old experts rapidly become obsolete.

Such issues, further complicated by international political rivalries, are behind the flaming debates over education. Following decades of emphasis on producing sociability specialists, interest has been reawakened in teaching of "hard subjects" to produce experts who can man technological posts. The debates dwell on virtually every aspect of education—the content of school curriculums, teaching methods, and school administration. Although the issues raised are far from new, ingredients of urgency and seriousness have been introduced that were missing in the previous decades and that have allowed persons from many walks of life to receive a hearing. For schools and, indeed, for educational machinery in general, this situation has created considerable strain. The sociologist tends to reject the layman's accusations of deliberate stalling tactics by incompetently trained educators with vested career interests. He similarly rejects educators' pleas that they alone are competent to judge educational processes. Instead, he regards schools as systems that have inherited functional obligations that may be obscured in the current debates but that are, nonetheless, embodied in the very structures of schools. Above all, in regarding schools as functioning systems he looks for equilibrating and sustaining mechanisms. In the following analysis this topic will be considered by attending to the fundamental theorem that we have already stated—an element of a system requires a degree of autonomy from that system if it is to make any functional contributions to that system.

Autonomy Processes within Schools

In addition to the autonomy dimensions characteristic of the internal organization of schools already outlined, there exists a body of research on existing autonomous processes in schools. These data focus mainly on children's relation to schools. The emphasis on the administrative levels thus far in this model is in keeping with sociological traditions about complex organizations; Weber's model included only administrative personnel. In recent years there have been debates as to whether workers in factories, clients of government agencies, or customers of stores really are part of their respective organizations. It is claimed in the present model that children are part of the school organization, but that their affiliation with schools is narrowly defined. Their opportunity for long affiliation with a school is severely curtailed, as is their opportunity for rising in the hierarchy—except the hierarchy that inexorably leads to departure from the school. In terms of autonomy patterns, the scope of the child's internal autonomy—that is, his autonomy in his role as pupil—is decidedly limited. But the intrusion into the school of his affiliations outside the school results in his external autonomy (autonomy external to his role as pupil) being enacted in the school. Much of the recent literature about youth culture can be thought of in these terms. Adolescents have active affiliations in a subculture that is separate from the world of adults but that nevertheless intrudes into the world of adults—into the home as well as into the school.

The school is not alone in having a category of participants who have a very limited form of affiliation with the organization but considerable external autonomy within the organization. Hospitals have patients who retain strong contact with their families while located in the hospitals. Factories have workers who have little opportunity for advancement but who can maintain a culture within the factory that is dissimilar from that of the administrative ranks and closely linked to the workingman's style of life outside the factory. Existing research findings may be roughly categorized as the "autonomous subcultures" and the "vicious cycle phenomenon."

Autonomous Subcultures   Burton Clark suggests that three types of subcultures can be found in schools: (1) the fun subculture; (2) the academic subculture; and (3) the delinquent subculture.[32] Teachers view the academic subculture as the group of serious students; Clark regards this subculture as relatively weak if not largely absent. Absent also are the rebellious intellectuals who are present in colleges. But Clark notes that "no one has bothered to report on how high school students support one another in serious work."[33]

Concerning the fun subculture, Coleman has found that

clothes, personal impressions, and cars are rated by children as highly important.[34] On the basis of a study of high-school girls, Clark notes:

> it is surprising that [academic success] does not count for more, because in some situations, the "stars," "heroes," and objects of adulation are those who best achieve the goals of the institution. For example, in the movie industry the leading crowd is composed of those who have achieved the top roles—they are by consensus the "stars." Or, in graduate school, the "leading crowd" of students ordinarily consists of bright students who excel in their studies. Not so for these high school girls. The leading crowd seems to be defined primarily in terms of *social* success: their personality, beauty, clothes—and in communities where social success is tied closely to family background, their money and family are important, too.[35]

Clark summarizes by pointing out that "it is clear from all these data [that] the interests of teenagers are not focused around studies." [36] This is true even in well-to-do suburbs where the high schools attempt to be academically oriented. In fact, frequently "special effort towards scholastic success may be *negatively* valued." [37]

Coleman's study emphasizes the difference between the values of high school students and those of the school. Investigation is needed, however, to determine whether the existence of divergent values, and adherence to these divergent values, means the existence of social conflict and, if so, the precise nature of such conflict. Could it be, for example, that the fun subculture and the academic supraculture are in some way mutually supportive? The study by Wayne Gordon that Clark cites supports this latter view, as does Willard Waller's earlier work in 1932.[38] Gordon suggests that the athletic portion of the fun subculture serves certain interests of the school.[39] It is (1) a form of control of the student because it channels adolescent energy away from tabooed areas; (2) a way of promoting school cohesion;[40] and (3) a public relations agent for the school toward the community (the marching band, glee club, and so on) that helps to draw the community into the school's affairs. "The local community typically 'participates' in the extra curricular activities in ways it cannot—or has not—in the curricular [activities]." [41]

A general adolescent culture is believed to exist "that extends across the nation" and gives sustenance to the high school subculture.

> This youth culture has growing support from institutions which operate apart from the parent, church, and the school in shaping the young; the young are hooked into the mass media and their adjuncts, from nursery level television programs to the movie to the disc jockey and juke box. These means of communication leap over other forms of social contact in affecting the style and content of the general youth culture. Their effectiveness is shown in the national crazes that race through the homes and haunts of the teen-agers. The rapidity of communication and the adaptation with the subworld of the young can be baffling to their elders, and is another point of tension between the generations.[42]

This suggests that youth culture needs to be viewed as a supraschool and suprahome system. Indeed, it may be regarded as a type of community. Don Martindale, among many others, has pointed out that the concept of community has undergone change in the Western world. He sees community as the "stabilization of solutions to collective problems" [43] and documents the transition from rural-village to urban to national community. This view differs from that of scholars who see the passing of the rural small community as the end of community and who see urban, cosmopolitan, and national social patterns as utterly diffuse and uncoordinated. By contrast, Martindale sees the emergence of different types of communities characterized by different social structures. The present author also approached this idea in his characterization of contact networks as forms of association that, without demanding extensive previous relationships, use mass communications as means of contact with many persons.[44]

In a parallel characterization the adolescent system may be seen as a peer-stimulation network in which there is contact without deep personal involvement. Such a system is highly adapted to the speed and capsulated content of mass communications. There is little harnessing of the communication pattern to traditional social positions and the responsibilities that these entail, especially that of subservience to adults. The suggestion here is that this peer system needs to be viewed as an autonomous system in its own right. It intrudes into the high school but is essentially divergent from it. It follows that the peer fun subculture in schools is not necessarily focused directly on opposition to schools or even toward conflict with schools but rather toward its own orientation, which is different from that of the school. The relation between the adolescent and the school is probably more nearly one of indifference than one of hostile opposition.

The delinquent subculture aims at "avoiding or rebelling against the whole enterprise. . . . Most students who are seriously delinquent want to get out of school." [45] There is active hostility to adults and to most other students, and there is challenge to authority. "They don't merely evade rules . . . they *flout* them." [46] The delinquent subculture creates discipline problems for teachers and is a threat to the traditional mandate of schools. Although it is obvious that teachers must see the action of these students as opposition to the school, it needs to be noted that the focus of opposition is obviously *not* the school, but the adult world, the world of authority that goes far beyond the school. In this sense there exists a quest for autonomy from the school, though the school is not the real enemy. When criminality is organized, as in juvenile gangs, it becomes an autonomous system with fairly clearly formalized structure. These systems intrude into schools but are actually intended to establish separate social structures that become the base from which operations are conducted.

The Vicious Cycle Phenomenon   Laymen as well as social scientists have long observed that some behavioral processes seem to perpetuate themselves from their own momentum so that, once set in motion, a train of activity develops that seemingly cannot be stopped. W. I. Thomas and Merton have written about this phenomenon. Thomas emphasized the definition of situations affecting human actions, and Merton refined this conception in an analysis of "self-fulfilling prophecies." [47] In somewhat more contemporary language one might speak of feedback systems that, under certain conditions, will produce a stability from which there is no escape; each element of the system serves further to stabilize the system. This situation is familiarly known as a vicious cycle. The concept of autonomy will, it is believed, contribute to clarification of the conditions that are involved in the stable feedback process of the self-fulfilling prophecy.

Perhaps the best-known examples of vicious cycles in school affairs can be seen in the impact of social-class membership. Traditionally, lower-class persons have had negative attitudes about the importance of education (this may well be changing) that have led them to drop out of school as early as possible. Their lack of education has, in turn, contributed to keeping them in the lower classes. More concretely, lower-class children's lack of educational motivation causes teachers to react negatively to them. The teachers' loss of interest in these children and lowered aspirations for them foster the lack of motivation of the children. Again, teaching in lower-class neighborhoods is defined as unattractive and unrewarding by the middle-class teacher, and middle-class-oriented teachers seem to dominate American schools. Teachers therefore seek transfers to "better" neighborhoods and leave the lower classes perpetually saddled with inexperienced teachers. This, in turn, perpetuates a lack of serious interest in either teaching or learning at this level.[48]

Each of the above sequences is obviously a stable feedback system. Each involves the interplay of a series of elements in a fixed interrelationship. Iron chains of circumstances bind the school to existing status attributes that are external to the school. Yet it is a primary function of a system of democratic-equalitarian education to break the links of such chains. A raison d'être of the school as a separate organization is the removal of children and teachers from their existing social contexts so that education can proceed in a setting that is relatively autonomous in its concentration upon educational functions.

From a practical point of view, the destruction of the vicious cycle involves the assertion of the autonomy of the school over that of the rival, cross-affiliational autonomies. Clark cites instances of schools being established for the purpose of deliberately emphasizing the dominance of academic subject matter.[49] He gives findings that show that, when sufficient autonomy is concentrated in schools, the rival autonomies can be counteracted; the lower-class child can be as strongly motivated to do well academically as the middle- and upper-class child.

The Control of Schools

Schools are organizations that perform specialized services, and these services are of vital and immediate interest to many segments of the community. Inherently this condition involves dilemmas of how the school is to accede to external, community pressures while operating effectively as a goal-directed social organization.[50] Clark states that the operational autonomy of schools is a critical factor in educational performance. Whether they are active centers of innovation (so necessary in a changing, expert society) or "passive instruments of other institutions" depends heavily on their freedom from subservience to outside agencies. Clark further states that

> the American public schools have relatively little independence since they are an extreme case of control by local citizens. . . . The local control system . . . renders the school heavily dependent on the wishes of the various political factions, churches, business groups, trade unions and the like that comprise the power structure of the local town or city . . ." [51]

Because the school is so vulnerable to local pressures, it is "an *accommodating* institution."

Clark suggests that there are three principles of authority present in American education. The first is public trust. "Long a part of the American tradition [is the belief] that schools and colleges should be directed ultimately by community interests rather than by professional personnel or government departments." Public trust has led to lay school boards made up of part-time amateur educators who are public representatives. In turn, it vitiates control by the state as well as by education departments comprised of education specialists. It decidedly reduces the school's autonomy as a separate system because it permits the intrusion of outside forces into the school's policy making. Bureaucratic authority is the second principle. Lay boards "are removed from actual operation while officials—full time, expert, informed—are on the spot, making daily decisions." Much determination of policy actually falls into their hands. Bureaucratic patterns of authority are increasingly used as schools get bigger and require expertise in their administrative staff. Also, community board members generally accept this model. Clark states that "many board members take a business firm [as the model] of how to organize the school or college. This conception stresses clear lines of authority and sharply demarcated jurisdictions for which officials are held responsible." The last principle is colleague authority. In higher education this principle tends to be dominant because it leads to strengthened control by the faculty. It implies a relatively low degree of power by the administration and emphasizes academic freedom.[52] Clark feels that grade schools and high schools are leaning toward the third type because they, too, rely increasingly on large professional staffs, and the teachers themselves are increasingly concerned with gaining professional status.

On the basis of debates over "Who runs the schools," [53] it would seem that there exist ill-defined optimums of school autonomy with respect to compliance with external pressures. How much autonomy must schools have to be effective as teaching centers? How much attunement to community pressure is necessary for schools to fulfill their mission in a democratic setting? At what point will the school's loss of autonomy destroy its usefulness as a separate socializing agency? One would wish to condense these questions into empirically manageable variables and to conduct experimental studies. The object of such research would be to establish optimal autonomy specifications for various types of educational processes, just as the theoretically-oriented engineer develops specifications for tolerances in mechanical equipment.

NOTES ...

1. See Neal Gross, "The Sociology of Education," *Sociology Today: Problems and Prospects*, Robert K. Merton, Leonard Broom, and L. S. Cottrell, Jr., eds. (New York: Basic Books, 1959), pp. 128–152; Neal Gross, "Some Contributions of Sociology to the Field of Education," *Harvard Educational Review*, XXIX (1959), 275–

287; W. W. Charters, Jr., "The School as a Social System," *Education and Research*, XXII (1962), 41–50; R. J. Havighurst and B. L. Neugarten, *Society and Education* (Boston: Allyn and Bacon, 1962); Peter M. Blau and W. R. Scott, *Formal Organizations* (San Francisco: Chandler, 1962); Amitai Etzioni, *A Comparative Analysis of Complex Organizations* (New York: Free Press, 1961).

2. Gouldner and Selznick are particularly clear in focusing on the pressures that impinge on organizations. See Alvin W. Gouldner, "Reciprocity and Autonomy in Functional Theory," *Symposium in Social Theory*, L. Gross, ed. (Evanston: Row, Peterson, 1959), pp. 241–270; P. Selznick, *TVA and the Grass Roots* (Berkeley: University of California Press, 1949).

3. This contrasts with nonsociological theories—notably H. A. Simon's decision-making approach to complex organizations—which relegate sociological variables to a somewhat secondary place. See Herbert A. Simon, "Decision-Making and Administrative Organization," *Public Administration Review*, IV (1944), 16–25, and *Administrative Behavior: A Study of Decision-Making Processes in Administrative Organizations* (New York: Macmillan, 1950).

4. Fritz J. Roethlisberger and William J. Dickson, *Management and the Worker* (Cambridge: Harvard University Press, 1939).

5. Peter M. Blau, *The Dynamics of Bureaucracy* (Chicago: University of Chicago Press, 1955).

6. Talcott Parsons, "Suggestions for a Sociological Approach to the Theory of Organizations," *Complex Organizations: A Sociological Reader*, Amitai Etzioni, ed. (New York: Holt, Rinehart and Winston, 1961), p. 33.

7. *Ibid.*, p. 35.

8. Blau and Scott, *Formal Organizations*, p. 5.

9. Alvin W. Gouldner, "Organizational Analysis," *Sociology Today: Problems and Prospects*, Merton, Broom, and Cottrell, Jr., eds. (New York: Basic Books, 1959).

10. *Ibid.*, p. 423.

11. *Webster's New Collegiate Dictionary* (Springfield, Mass.: 1954).

12. *Ibid.*

13. Features not discussed are problems of measuring autonomy and of autonomy as a component of personality structure. For a study that focuses on autonomy with reference to personality of mem-

bers of social organizations, see Bruno Bettelheim, *The Informed Heart: Autonomy in a Mass Age* (New York: Free Press, 1960). Bettelheim's book deals with inmates of concentration camps.

14. Parsons, "Suggestions for a Sociological Approach to the Theory of Organizations," p. 34.

15. Israel Gerver and Joseph Bensman, "Toward a Sociology of Expertness," *Social Forces*, XXXII (1954), 226–235.

16. Blau and Scott, *Formal Organizations*, pp. 35–36.

17. Personal communication from Paul C. Rosenblatt.

18. Chester I. Barnard, *The Functions of the Executive* (Cambridge: Harvard University Press, 1946).

19. Robert K. Merton, *Social Theory and Social Structure* (New York: Free Press, 1957), pp. 131–160.

20. S. M. Lipset, "Bureaucracy and Social Reform," *Complex Organizations: A Sociological Reader*, pp. 264–265.

21. There exist, however, suggestive ideas in the work of Chester Barnard. Barnard, who was himself an executive, poses a conception of administration that allows considerable autonomy among rank-and-file members. He notes that conflicting loyalties are unavoidable and that the individual's "willingness to serve" is a crucial item in the organization's structure. He also notes that administrative functions are served by executives being involved in informal interaction: they have access to information without having to act officially on this information. Executives have access to "communication of intangible facts, opinions, suggestions, suspicions, that cannot pass through formal channels without raising issues calling for decisions, without dissipating dignity and objective authority, and without overloading executive positions" (Barnard, *The Functions of the Executive*, pp. 100 ff., 225).

22. W. J. Goode, "Family Disorganization," *Contemporary Social Problems*, Robert K. Merton and R. A. Nisbet, eds. (New York: Harcourt, Brace, 1961), p. 393.

23. See, for example, A. B. Hollingshead, *Elmtown's Youth* (New York: Wiley, 1949); Havighurst and Neugarten, *Society and Education*.

24. Charters, "The School as a Social System."

25. Blau and Scott, *Formal Organizations*, pp. 51 ff.

26. Talcott Parsons, "The Professions and Social Structure," *Essays in Sociological Theory*, rev. ed. (New York: Free Press, 1954).

27. Fred E. Katz and H. W. Martin, "Career Choice Processes," *Social Forces*, XLI (1963), 149–154.

28. J. S. Coleman, *The Adolescent Society* (New York: Free Press, 1961).

29. Alvin W. Gouldner, "Cosmopolitans and Locals: Toward an Analysis of Latent Social Roles," *Administrative Science Quarterly*, II (1957), 281–306.

30. Parsons, "Suggestions for a Sociological Approach to the Theory of Organizations."

31. Emile Durkheim, *The Division of Labor in Society*, George Simpson, tr. (New York: Free Press, 1947).

32. Burton R. Clark, *Educating the Expert Society* (San Francisco: Chandler, 1962).

33. *Ibid.*, p. 245.

34. Coleman, *The Adolescent Society*.

35. Clark, *Educating the Expert Society*, p. 249.

36. *Ibid.*, p. 251, Chaps. III and IV.

37. *Ibid.*, p. 252.

38. Willard Waller, *The Sociology of Teaching* (New York: Wiley, 1932).

39. Clark, *Educating the Expert Society*, pp. 254 ff.

40. Waller, *The Sociology of Teaching*, pp. 112 ff. According to Waller, athletics unify the school by promoting a united effort against a common external enemy.

41. Clark, *Educating the Expert Society*, pp. 255–256.

42. *Ibid.*, pp. 256–257.

43. Don Martindale, *American Society* (New York: Van Nostrand, 1960), pp. 165 ff.

44. Fred E. Katz, "Occupational Contact Networks," *Social Forces*, XXXVII (1958), 52–55.

45. Clark, *Educating the Expert Society*, pp. 262, 263.

46. *Ibid.*, p. 263.

47. Merton, *Social Theory and Social Structure*, Chap. XI.

48. Clark, *Educating the Expert Society*, pp. 96 ff.

49. *Ibid.*, pp. 261–263.

50. Neal Gross's study of the lack of consensus regarding the role of the school superintendent is an example of the existence of poten-

tial cross-pressures on school systems. See N. Gross, *Explorations in Role Analysis: Studies of the School Superintendency Role* (New York: Wiley, 1958)

51. Clark, *Educating the Expert Society*, pp. 40–41.

52. *Ibid.*, pp. 152–154.

53. Neal Gross, *Who Runs Our Schools?* (New York: Wiley, 1958).

2

Integrative and Adaptive
Uses of Autonomy:
Worker Autonomy in Factories

A generation after the well-known Hawthorne studies,[1] no one questions the existence of informal groups in complex organizations. Numerous studies have documented their existence, especially among employees in the lowest ranks. But the task remains of developing an adequate *conceptual* explanation of how persons in the lowest ranks, having limited career prospects in their work and slight opportunity for advancement, are incorporated into work organizations on a relatively permanent basis. In other words, how can we account for the integration of organizations that include a large number of persons who are largely disenfranchised from the organization's reward system? How can we account for the apparent collaboration, if not loyalty, of persons who, since the time of Marx, have been described as being alienated from their work?[2] A brief, though oversimplified, answer is that workers need work and factories need workers. We can hardly argue with this statement. Yet the economic interdependence of workers and factories does not clarify the nature of the structural arrangement under which the interdependence is worked out.

The proposed answer to the question of how workers are incorporated into complex organizations has two aspects. First, workers have considerable autonomy within the confines of the organization. Even when their work is prescribed in exact detail, the work role tends to be defined narrowly. This situation leaves a considerable portion of the worker's life within the work organization *undefined*. Second, workers tend to use this autonomy to bring their working-class culture into the organization, even though it is alien to the bureaucratic ethos of the higher echelons of the organization. This practice produces continuity between the workman's outside life and his participation in the work setting—a setting to which he has very limited allegiance.[3] This continuity in turn promotes workers' integration into work organizations.

The guiding perspective of our study is that the culture of informal work groups is a manifestation of autonomy within the confines of the organization and that autonomy is an aspect of organizational structure even as it was in the schools. Autonomy, defined as independence from external control, means in this case that the activities of workers within the organization are not fully controlled by the organization. There is, therefore, scope for the development of various informal patterns: some patterns lessen the boredom of workers and in other ways help get work done; others are contrary to the goals of the organization. Autonomy can be considered as an aspect of the very structure of the organization, which materializes as spheres of independence delegated directly or indirectly by the organization. Directly delegated autonomy refers to specific rules that delimit an area of independence; for example, a rule specifying that the foreman can decide who will work the night shift indicates a sphere in which the foreman has autonomy, one in which he exercises discretion. By contrast, indirect delegation of autonomy results from the absence of rules; in a sphere where no clear rules exist, autonomy exists by default. Both direct and indirect delegation of autonomy promote spheres of activity that are not closely controlled by the organization. Our thesis is that the resulting autonomous behavior must be considered as an aspect of organizational structure, not merely as deviance from it. In the main, this chapter will examine autonomy based on indirect delegation, since this aspect seems to characterize informal patterns among workers.

Worker autonomy can be regarded as part of the barter arrangement between workers and the organization, in which limited affiliation with the organization is exchanged for a degree of autonomy. The arrangement has important adaptive functions for both parties. For the organization it is a way of promoting the affiliation of some of its employees with the organization, while at the same time excluding them from certain vital spheres of organizational activity. For workers it permits continuation of the working-class style of life and provides ties of sociability in a context that in many ways is alien to the workman's culture. In short, the autonomy appears to have adaptive and pattern-maintenance functions for the workers and adaptive and goal-attainment functions for the organization. It must be noted that worker autonomy, although enacted *in* the work organization, is essentially *external* to his work role. Worker autonomy thus contrasts with the autonomy pattern for white-collar workers, that is, for all those who, from the lowliest clerk to the president, make up the administrative hierarchy. They have greater autonomy *within* their work role, but their role is more broadly defined than that of the worker. This way of analyzing roles was developed more fully in Chapter 1. In the case of the white-collar worker it means taking his work role *outside* the organization; for the blue-collar worker, it means bringing his nonwork role *into* the organization.

The term "autonomy" here covers much of the same ground that is now covered by the term "informal organization." However, the present way of looking at autonomy tries to eliminate some of the ambiguities in the distinction between informal organization and formal organization. Herbert A. Simon and his colleagues summarize the existing distinction.[4] Formal organization is defined as "a planned system of cooperative effort in which each participant has a recognized role to play and duties or tasks to perform."[5] Informal organization is defined as "the whole pattern of actual behavior—the way members of the organization really do behave —insofar as these actual behaviors do not coincide with the formal plan." [6] Research findings support the idea that the formal organization is made up of a planned system and informal organization of actual behavior that deviates from the formal plans. But the research procedures themselves seem to lay the groundwork for producing these findings. The very nature of the research strategies promotes the search for deviance where informal patterns are concerned and the assumption of legitimacy where the formal patterns are concerned.

The explicit rules of formal organization do not prescribe informal behavior patterns; therefore, informal behavior must be discovered through direct, detailed investigation and observation. This kind of research is likely to dwell on actual behavior of people rather than abstract rules, on collaboration on the local level among the interacting people rather than collaboration with the total organization. All this is likely to show innovation and departure from rules rather than compliance with rules. The findings resulting from this emphasis in the research process tend to perpetuate the initial contention that informal patterns deviate from the planned system, thereby creating a self-fulfilling prophecy. As a result, despite evidence that informal patterns may be very firmly established within an organization,[7] the view persists that informal patterns lack legitimacy and permanence. If the behavior patterns that are relevant to formal structure were subjected to similarly detailed observational scrutiny, a picture might emerge that is far closer to so-called informal patterns than we now have.[8] It is noteworthy that when studying "planned" patterns, researchers usually omit the behavior involved in the *planning* of these patterns!

To define the difference between formal organization and informal organization as that between a planned system and actual behavior is theoretically weak. Actual behavior is undoubtedly relevant to planned systems; and system characteristics, even planned ones, are relevant to actual behavior. The distinction seems to need refocusing to enable orderly analysis of structure and behavior. The following formulation should help to clarify the situation: *Organizational structure includes relatively controlled and relatively autonomous spheres.* The controlled sphere can include both direct and indirect specification of behavior; similarly, the autonomous sphere can include directly and indirectly specified behavior. Table 2 offers an application of this approach by giving an idealized comparison of the way the roles of executive and blue-collar worker are structured. Each role contains spheres of autonomy and spheres of controlled behavior. The executive's role contains autonomy within his organizational tasks. His role is defined by broad rules that serve as guidelines to his behavior but do not define closely which particular acts he must perform. The rules specify the areas in which he has flexibility. On the other hand, this is an indirect way of specifying control over him: He *must* comply with the guidelines, but his compliance can be assessed only by judging how he uses his flexibility. The blue-collar worker, on the other hand, has very little autonomy in his work, since his tasks tend to be specified in detail. But this leaves him with opportunity to engage in nonwork behavior, which is not specified by his organizational task responsibilities.

The traditional conception of formal patterns parallels the "controlled" spheres (cells 3 and 4 in Table 2). In the present approach both "formal" and "informal" are subsumed under analytical categories that conceptualize both in comparable terms. No longer are informal patterns merely stubbornly recurring residual patterns within a formalized scheme of organizational structure.

The writings of Chester I. Barnard illustrate that autonomous and controlled behavior coexist within organizations and that the

Table 2. Structural Components of the Roles of Executives and Blue-Collar Workers

	Directly Specified Behavior	Indirectly Specified Behavior
Spheres of Autonomous Behavior	*Executive Role:* Rules act as broad guidelines to behavior, specify areas of autonomy within organizational tasks. 1	*Blue-Collar Worker Role:* Narrowly defined tasks permit autonomy to exist externally to work tasks, yet enacted *in* the organization. 2
Spheres of Controlled Behavior	*Blue-Collar Worker Role:* Tasks are governed by detailed specifications. 4	*Executive Role:* Rules set *limits* to autonomy; adherence to the limits is judged by executive's use of autonomy. 3

executive must fuse them.[9] Barnard notes that autonomy among personnel is not necessarily detrimental to executive control but may, in fact, be an asset to administrative processes. He suggests that the executive must rely on the "willingness to serve" [10] of those under his command; he must recognize that there is a "zone of indifference" [11] in which persons are prepared to accept orders but beyond which they are apt to oppose orders. Informal patterns, in Barnard's view of the executive, are not divisive forces but "expansions of the means of communication with reduction in the necessity for formal decisions, the minimizing of undesirable influences, and the promotion of desirable influences concordant with the scheme of formal responsibilities." [12] From Barnard's perspective both formal and informal patterns can be harnessed in the service of a "co-operating system." It seems, however, that the real point is not the blending of formally and informally organized behaviors, but the blending of controlled and autonomous behaviors that exist within organizations. Barnard's model of the organization is filled with autonomy patterns that can serve the whole organization; some of these patterns proceed from direct official specification of behavior and some come from indirect specification.

The Worker's Place in the Organization

Workers are viewed here as being permitted to develop relatively autonomous subcultures and subsystems of social interaction in their day-to-day routines. The autonomous patterns diverge from the officially prescribed patterns but are very much in line with the workman's style of life and culture outside the organization. The culture of the working-class man is in many ways alien to the decorum and demeanor expected of white-collar members of the organization. In the routinized work of the white-collar worker there is no room for the sudden display of anger of the working-class male; for the white-collar worker who meets the public there is little scope for the pervasive sexual allusions of the working-class male. Yet within the working clique inside the organization, the workman can enact the culture patterns of his life outside the organization. He can, for example, indulge freely in what is perhaps one of the workman's major forms of creative mental activity: the verbal play, imaginative exploits, and romanticism on the theme of sex. This does not mean that middle and upper-class males do not engage in this form of mental sport, but merely that for the working-class male it seems to be a *major* creative outlet, and much less so for the middle and upper classes. The workman's pattern is made possible by the fact that he has a large sphere of verbal freedom, since much of what he says "doesn't count," as far as his work is concerned. Unlike the white-collar worker, whose work consists of a world of words, written and spoken, the worker is basically measured by the contributions of his hands. Therefore, his verbal jostlings, such as the razzing of the lowest person on the prestige totem pole, are not considered part of his job. As will be shown in the review of Donald F. Roy's study, the content of the workman's verbal banter is related to his niche in the social order and the conditions of his social existence.[13] The same relationship is also reflected in patterns of practical jokes and prankish physical contact, which are characteristic of the workman's culture but taboo in the culture of the white-collar worker. Participating in physical contact—be it fighting, prankish shoving, or contact sports —is chiefly characteristic of male preadult culture. Presumably it is only at the low socio-economic levels that this pattern continues into adulthood.

By contrast, the white-collar workers, whether senior executives or junior administrators, have a broad affinity for the organizational style of behavior. They are likely to be members of the middle or upper class, where they have learned the demeanor and proprieties of manner they will be expected to exercise in their position in the organization. There is little discrepancy, for instance, between the style of dress and speech of their social class and that associated with the bureaucratic style of behavior. White-collar workers can apply elements of their external life to their job in the organization without having to make fundamental adjustments in their general style of behavior, although this does not mean that they have nothing to learn in their work. The thesis of the organization man makes the same point in converse terms: The work habits and interests of the white-collar worker spill over into his family and community life. For the white-collar worker, the organization is less clearly differentiated from the culture of his private world than it is for the worker; the organization is not the enemy camp. The blue-collar worker, on the other hand, is eager to leave his work behind him as he leaves the gates of the factory.[14]

In sum, white-collar workers have greater autonomy *in their task-related activities* than do the blue-collar workers. The time clock, the regimentation involved in feeding a machine and gearing one's work to the pace of a machine, the necessity of doing one's work exclusively at the location of a particular machine apply to the blue-collar worker to a far larger extent than to the white-collar worker. For the latter, work is defined more broadly than it is for the blue-collar worker, requiring a more diffuse commitment. Thus, for the white-collar worker, a broad range of activities and personal attributes, from personal grooming to getting along with others, are defined as relevant to work. A good organization man's allegiance to the organization and its style of action include taking part in such activities as organizing a Little League baseball team, helping with the local community chest drive, and participating in college alumni affairs after working hours. And he must communicate his outside interests to his work peers. It is difficult to assess which activities are regarded as clearly *external* to his work role. On the other hand, the worker's tasks are defined more narrowly, leaving scope for activity that is defined as *external* to his work to be enacted while he is at his place of work.

The limited bases for the worker's *allegiance* to the work organization are tacitly recognized not only by the exclusion of the worker from administrative decision making but also by his being allowed to bring into the work setting working-class culture patterns and to fashion them into relatively autonomous subcultures. In short, the worker's external affiliations with the working-class style of life are permitted to intrude into the organization that employs him. This can be viewed as part of the exchange (in addition to monetary pay) for the limited forms of reward and participation that the worker is given by the employing organization. In view of the differentiation between worker subculture and bureaucratic culture, the worker's immersion in working-class patterns may serve to perpetuate his disenfranchisement from the administrative sphere, resulting in a vicious cycle.

The pattern pictured thus far, of workers in relation to factory, is chiefly characteristic of the modern Western world. A contrasting example exists in the Japanese pattern, where the worker is expected to make a lifetime commitment to one firm.[15] The worker does not expect to leave his initial place of employment—the idea of moving to a better job seems highly incongruous. The firm does not intend to dismiss employees, no matter how uneconomical it may be to keep them. In this arrangement the worker's affiliation with the firm is a relatively complete one, and there appears to be little external autonomy.

Enactment of Worker Autonomy: An Example

The empirical study of workers in factories has been a favorite of sociologists and social psychologists. Among the most eloquently descriptive studies of the culture and interaction patterns of workers are those by Roy. In " 'Banana Time' . . ." Roy describes a small work group of men engaged in the exceedingly simple manual work of operating a punch press.[16] It took about fifteen minutes to learn this work. Roy himself participated, and his description shows his intimate immersion in the field situation as well as his keen observational skills. Roy describes how he attempted, during the early days of work, to meet the problems of great boredom by inventing little games. He partly succeeded. After a while he noticed that the bantering and "kidding" by the workers around him were not purely haphazard, but actually served a similar function as his games; they, too, reduced boredom. Following this insight he made systematic studies and discovered *patterns* in the bantering and joking.

> What I saw at first, before I began to observe, was occasional flurries of horse-play so simple and unvarying in pattern and so childish in quality that they made no strong bid for attention. For example, Ike would regularly switch off the power at Sammy's machine whenever Sammy made a trip to the lavatory or the drinking fountain. Correlatively, Sammy invariably fell victim to the

plot by making an attempt to operate his clicking hammer after returning to the shop. And, as the simple pattern went, this blind stumbling into the trap was always followed by indignation and reproach from Sammy, smirking satisfaction from Ike, and mild paternal scolding from George. My interest in this procedure was at first confined to wondering when Ike would weary of his tedious joke or when Sammy would learn to check his power switch before trying the hammer. But, as I began to pay closer attention, as I began to develop familiarity with the communication system, the disconnected became connected, the nonsense made sense, the obscure became clear, and the silly actually funny. And, as the content of the interaction took on more and more meaning, the interaction began to reveal structure.[17]

Roy discovered that the day's routine was broken by activities other than those formally instituted by the company or those which were "idiosyncratically developed disjunctions." There were also an "ordered series of informal interactions." Roy describes many forms of interruption that took place and the patterning involved in them. One of these was "peach time," when one worker, Sammy, provided a peach and shared it. His beneficiaries greeted his contribution with disgruntlement and complaints about the quality of the peach. "Banana time" followed.

Banana time followed peach time by approximately an hour. Sammy again provided the refreshments, namely, one banana. There was, however, no four-way sharing of Sammy's banana. Ike would gulp it down by himself after surreptitiously extracting it from Sammy's lunch box, kept on a shelf behind Sammy's work station. Each morning, after making the snatch, Ike would call out, "Banana time!" and proceed to down his prize, while Sammy made futile protests and denunciations. George would join in with mild remonstrances, sometimes scolding Sammy for making so much fuss. The banana was one which Sammy brought for his own consumption at lunch time; he never did get to eat his banana, but kept bringing one for his lunch. At first this daily theft startled and amazed me. Then I grew to look forward to the daily seizure and the verbal interaction that followed.[18]

In addition to peach time and banana time there were coffee time, fish time, coke time, lunch time, and window-opening time. Each of them was marked by a distinctive pattern of interaction. In addition to these patterned times, Roy notes themes in verbal interplay.

> The themes had become standardized in their repetition. . . . Topics of conversation ranged in quality from an extreme of non-sensical chatter to another extreme of serious discourse. Unlike the times, these themes flowed one into the other in no particular sequence of predictability. Serious conversation could suddenly melt into horse play, and vice versa. In the middle of a serious discussion on the high cost of living, Ike might drop a weight be-hind the easily startled Sammy or hit him over the head with a dusty paper sack. Interaction would immediately drop to a low comedy exchange of slaps, threats, guffaws, and disapprobations.[19]

In this verbal interplay exaggeration was a common feature. For instance, one of the men had received one hundred dollars from his son; from that day he was seen as a man ready to retire with a sizable, steady income. Roy, after having admitted that he owned two acres of land, became a large landowner, and his farm became populated with horses, cows, pigs, and chickens. Sexuality also came in for a large share of regular and inventive verbal play.

Roy's article is perhaps a culmination in a series of research findings that, since the days of the Hawthorne studies, have pointed to the demise of the economic man without, however, completing the task of making social organization the focus of analysis. The early studies opposed the economic-man thesis by pointing out that the individual was not guided only by his own monetary self-interest. Indeed, he could be guided against his own self-interest by his worker peer group; the individual worker might actually lose income by following the output control patterns of his peers. It was emphasized that there was a "group factor" in work situa-tions; but still an individualistic, social psychological focus was retained for this group factor. In the Hawthorne studies there was much concern with changes in attitude toward work. The meaning of work was considered a basic factor in individuals' performance, and work groups were considered in molding the meaning and attitudes for members of the group.[20] Roy's interpretation of his findings is similarly social-psychological. To him, the informal patterns serve primarily to provide job satisfaction by relieving boredom. Along with many students of industrial relations in the last thirty years, he notes the existence of relatively distinct subgroups that are separate from the formal structure in the factory and have relatively distinct culture and interaction patterns. Yet his basic interpretation is in individualistic, psychological terminology—it relieves boredom. Even if one accepts the psychological perspective, one must question whether routine, repetitive work is necessarily conducive to boredom. For example, Ely Chinoy's study of automobile assembly-line workers suggests that workers' response to routine, repetitive work is perhaps better characterized by irritation at their lack of control over their work than by boredom.[21] To understand this feature, it is not necessary to conclude that repetitive activity necessarily leads to boredom; rather, one must allow for the influence of culture. The researcher may exaggerate the activistic theme of Western societies. The Jicarilla Apache, for example, "have an infinite capacity for not being bored. They can sit for hours on end and apparently do nothing; they certainly don't intellectualize about doing nothing." [22]

On the basis of Roy's evidence that *considerable structuring of the work situation is done by the workers themselves,* attention will be directed to the autonomy that is enjoyed by the work group and that seems to be a basic feature in the social organization of the work situation. Concentrating on autonomy structure does not completely avoid the danger of overemphasizing one set of structures and one set of functions, just as social-psychological studies have done. But it should help to broaden the existing perspective. As Roy describes it, the work situation in the autonomous group culture includes a great variety of behaviors that are not directly connected with their work. Many of these types of behavior fit Georg Simmel's description of play forms of social reality.[23] Subjects that are of serious concern, such as economic security, sexual virility, health and death, submission to the authority of other men, family loyalty, and status aspirations are examined in a context where they are stripped of their serious content. Flitting from one topic to another—from the deeply serious to the comic, from the immediately practical to the remotely romantic—implies an irrelevance of the practical, concrete reality in which each of the subjects is, in fact, embedded. Perhaps it is because members are simultaneously engaged in serious work that they feel free to treat other concerns in such a detached manner. Roy's group appears to be a veritable haven for the enactment of play forms. Elements of life that are largely beyond the control of the individual are exposed and, in a fashion, dealt with. The verbal themes are the clearest evidence of this area of enactment. In addition to play forms, it may well be that the various social interaction patterns—the "razzing" of Sammy, the paternalism of George—are reiterations of serious realities in the larger social context in which the men find themselves. Notice that it is Sammy, the newest immigrant (all three men are immigrants) who is the scapegoat; it is George, the only Gentile, who quietly occupies the superior status; it is the Negro handyman who is the object of stereotypical banter about uncontrolled sexuality.

These elements, whether they are fairly explicit reiterations or play forms of the workman's life outside the factory, are continuities between life outside the factory and life inside the factory and, therefore, are important for understanding the nature of the bond between the worker and the organization in which he is employed. Work peers participate in a common culture that relies heavily on their common fate both within and outside the organization. By means of their commonality they retain a fundamental alienation from the white-collar ranks in the organization. This condition is demonstrated in Chinoy's findings of workers' widespread lack of interest in becoming foremen or white-collar workers.[24] It is also supported by Charles R. Walker and Robert H. Guest's study of assembly-line workers. Walker and Guest found that workers were favorably disposed toward their immediate job but intensely dissatisfied with the factory as a whole.[25] Although there is a lack of affiliation with the white-collar ranks of the organization, the worker does form bonds within the organization with his own peers.[26] For the organization, this division of workers into two cultural groups permits an uneasy truce but also assures the continuity of the fundamental internal antithesis between the two. The dichotomy manifests itself in problems of morale and communications.

Roy points out that the group had developed a "full-blown

sociocultural system." The group was to a considerable extent a separate and distinct system in which the members had active, at times even creative, participation contrasting sharply with their minimal participation in the larger organization. *Work was not at all a major focus of this sociocultural system.* Recognition of this point gives a new perspective to the dilemma as to whether factory workers are strongly alienated from their work.[27] It appears that work was *one of a variety* of topics around which Roy's group had developed behavioral patterns, but work was by no means the central point of attention of this "full-blown sociocultural system."

The contention that work was not a central feature of Roy's work group differs considerably from traditional explanations of informal groups. It must be understood that the kind of data Roy presented have traditionally been interpreted largely in terms of their relevance to work. Typical statements would be to the effect that informal activities give meaning to dull, routine factory work[28] and that "work output is a function of the degree of work satisfaction, which in turn depends upon the informal social patterns of the work group." [29] These statements provide a social-psychological explanation of the groups' mediating effect between the individual and his work, but they do not provide an adequate structural explanation of the place of informal groups in a complex organization.

In addition to the social-psychological interpretations, there are well-documented studies by Roy and others that show production control and worker collusion by informal groups of workers against management.[30] In these cases there can be no doubt that informal patterns are relevant to work. But it is not certain, even here, that informal groups exist primarily for the worker's control over work or whether the explanation should not be reversed; that is, that control over work exists because of the presence of informal groups, which, in turn, exist because of the worker's relative autonomy.

In summary, it is suggested that Roy's work group exhibits a rich sociocultural system that is made possible by substantial worker autonomy. The autonomy exists by default; a worker's role is so narrowly defined that there remains a considerable sphere of undefined action within the confines of the organization. The con-

tent of the sociocultural system to which a worker belongs is made
up of a variety of elements from the culture and social context of
workers outside the factory. These elements manifest themselves
as direct reiterations as well as play forms of the reality. They
provide continuity between the workman's life outside the factory
and his participation within the factory.

In using the Roy study to illustrate autonomy patterns among
factory workers, certain cautionary statements must be made. The
group Roy studied may be atypical in its small amount of managerial supervision and in its degree of isolation from the rest of
the factory, so that it might be allowed a disproportionately high
degree of autonomy compared with other work groups. Further investigation would be required to demonstrate whether the Roy
group is typical or atypical. However, worker-autonomy structure
is evident from many other studies. For instance, Alvin W. Gouldner's discovery of a managerial "indulgency pattern" toward workers[31] and Joseph Bensman and Israel Gerver's finding of "deviancy
in maintaining the social system" in a factory[32] all point to distinctly structured worker autonomy.

Theoretical Considerations about Integration within Complex Organizations

Complex organizations must have ways of procuring and integrating
the services of a variety of participants. The process of procurement and integration can obviously be accomplished most readily
in organizations that have coercive means at their disposal. Prisons
can force inmates to peel potatoes. But organizations that do not
have coercion at their disposal are of particular interest, for there
can be little doubt that most noncoercive complex organizations
do, in fact, solve the problem.

The concern of this chapter has been the integration of a
particular segment of the membership of complex organizations,
namely, blue-collar workers in factories. It specifically faced up to
the vital question of how these persons are integrated into an
organization that offers them so few of the rewards that it can
bestow. The answer lies in a kind of federalism that governs the
situation. Workers are permitted ample separation from the total

organization, and to a considerable extent their integration into the larger system is left up to themselves. Informal work-group cultures are the concrete structures that make up the solution.

The separation of workers from the employing organization permits workers flexibility and options as to the degree of alienation from the whole organization. At the same time, the separation gives the organization freedom to adopt means and goals that are different from, if not alien to, those of the workers. The federalistic balance between the autonomy of the blue-collar workers and the autonomy of the white-collar staff allows flexibility to both sides. This dualism is also a potential source of divergence and conflict, which finds nurture in the separate subcultures.

In contrast to the form of integration suggested here, other writings have been concerned with developing models of organization that stress lessening internal differentiation. It is felt that the perceived divergence of interest between workers and the white-collar staff can and *needs to be* lessened if the organization is to operate effectively.[33] These writings differ from the present discussion both in theoretical and practical focuses. On the theoretical side, the above exposition is based on the view that autonomy can be viewed as a structural principle of organizations, which can have positive or negative consequences for their operation. Structured autonomy manifests itself in internal divergences, but these are not necessarily disruptive and maladaptive for the whole organization or any part of it. As to practical goals, many writers, notably W. F. Whyte and Chris Argyris,[34] are concerned with the problem of improving human relations in industrial concerns. In contrast, the practical focus here is not on improving social relationships in complex organizations; it is on the problem of improving the analytic theory of complex organizations. This is not necessarily a more worthy or pressing problem than that of improving human relationships in complex organizations; but it, too, is a problem.

In the present perspective, then, so-called informal patterns are facilitated by the existence of structurally guaranteed autonomy. That this is so does not make tension and strain inevitable. To be sure, informal patterns may give rise to hostile coalitions toward the organization, such as restriction of output; but they may also give rise to workers developing, on their own, forms of integration with the organization that are acceptable to that organization as well as to the workers themselves. The real point is that many adaptive functions of the total organization are delegated to the individual members of the organization by the mechanism of *not* being officially promulgated in a set of official rules.

NOTES ...

1. Fritz J. Roethlisberger and William J. Dickson, *Management and the Worker* (Cambridge: Harvard University Press, 1939).

2. For a survey and research application of the theme of worker alienation, see Robert Blauner, *Alienation and Freedom: The Factory Worker and His Industry* (Chicago: University of Chicago Press, 1964).

3. For a summary of the literature on the limited commitment of workers to the complex organizations in which they work, as well as to work itself, see Chris Argyris, *Integrating the Individual and the Organization* (New York: Wiley, 1964). In Part IV the author provides a summary of the debate as to whether the worker is alienated. Although Argyris' book is addressed to the same general issue as this chapter, his concern is the important one of developing organizational patterns so that there is congruence between the psychological needs of members and the administrative requirements of the organization. This chapter, in contrast, attempts to remain entirely on the level of social structure. See also Robert Dubin, "Industrial Workers' World: A Study of the 'Central Life Interests' of Industrial Workers," Erwin O. Smigel, ed., *Work and Leisure* (New Haven: College and University Press, 1963), pp. 53–72.

4. Herbert A. Simon, Donald W. Smithburg, and Victor Thompson, *Public Administration* (New York: Knopf, 1962).

5. *Ibid.*, p. 5.

6. *Ibid.*, p. 87.

7. Roethlisberger and Dickson, *Management and the Worker*. This classic report is still one of the most complete studies of informal groups. See also Peter M. Blau, "Structural Effects," *American Sociological Review*, XXV (1960), 178–193; also Peter M. Blau,

The Dynamics of Bureaucracy (Chicago: University of Chicago Press, 1955).

8. Indeed, Blau's work comes close to providing just such a picture; see Blau, *The Dynamics of Bureaucracy.*

9. Chester I. Barnard, *The Functions of the Executive* (Cambridge: Harvard University Press, 1938).

10. *Ibid.*, pp. 83 ff.

11. *Ibid.*, pp. 167 ff.

12. *Ibid.*, p. 227.

13. S. M. Miller and Frank Riesman suggest that the "factory 'horse-play,' " the "ritualistic kidding," are partly an expression of the working-class theme of person centeredness; see Miller and Riesman, "The Working-Class Subculture," *Blue Collar World*, A. B. Shostak and W. Gamberg, eds. (Englewood Cliffs, N.J.: Prentice-Hall, 1964), pp. 24–35.

14. Robert Blauner, "Occupational Differences in Work Satisfaction," *Social Organization and Behavior*, R. L. Simpson and I. H. Simpson, eds. (New York: Wiley, 1964), pp. 287–292.

15. James C. Abegglen, *The Japanese Factory: Aspects of Its Social Organization* (New York: Free Press, 1960). Opinion differs as to whether Abegglen's formulation about lifelong commitment applies to blue-collar workers in large factories.

16. Donald F. Roy, " 'Banana Time' Job Satisfaction and Informal Interaction," *Human Organization*, XVIII (1960), 158–168.

17. *Ibid.*, p. 161

18. *Ibid.*, p. 162.

19. *Ibid.*, p. 163.

20. Roethlisberger and Dickson, *Management and the Worker*; Edward Gross, *Work and Society* (New York: Crowell, 1958), Chap. XIV.

21. Ely Chinoy, *Automobile Workers and the American Dream* (New York: Random House, 1955)

22. Personal communication from H. Clyde Wilson.

23. *The Sociology of Georg Simmel*, K. H. Wolff, ed. and tr. (New York: Free Press, 1950), 43 ff.

24. Chinoy, *Automobile Workers and the American Dream*, especially Chap. V. See also, E. W. Bakke, *The Unemployed Worker* (New Haven: Yale University Press, 1940); and a poll conducted by

Fortune (May 1947), both cited by Chinoy. Chinoy's explanation of the lack of desire for promotion is that workers have become so discouraged in the course of their work careers that they have given up. He notes that workers are reacting to "the limited opportunities available, to the uncertainties stemming from the informal procedures by which foremen were chosen, and to the nature of the foreman's job itself" (p. 49). This explanation is not irreconcilable with the one offered here. The young factory worker, who does have visions of advancement, is presumably not sufficiently knowledgeable about the culture wall between himself and the administrative bureaucrat.

25. Charles R. Walker and Robert H. Guest, *The Man on the Assembly Line* (Cambridge: Harvard University Press, 1952), for example, pp. 139–140.

26. Dubin's studies suggest, however, that workers' friendship bonds with work peers are less important than bonds with peers outside the work setting; see Dubin, "Industrial Workers' World: A Study of the *'Central Life Interests'* of Industrial Workers."

27. Argyris believes that workers are strongly alienated (*Integrating the Individual and the Organization*); Walker and Guest point out in *The Man on the Assembly Line* that workers they studied were relatively contented doing simple, repetitive work.

28. Gross, *Work and Society.*

29. Reinhard Bendix and Lloyd H. Fisher, "The Perspectives of Elton Mayo," *Complex Organizations: A Sociological Reader*, Amitai Etzioni, ed. (New York: Holt, Rinehart and Winston, 1961), p. 119.

30. See Donald F. Roy, "Efficiency and 'The Fix': Informal Intergroup Relations in a Piecework Machine Shop," *Sociology: The Progress of a Decade*, S. M. Lipset and N. J. Smelser, eds. (Englewood Cliffs, N. J.: Prentice-Hall, 1961), pp. 378–390; also, Donald F. Roy, "Quota Restriction and Goldbricking in a Machine Shop," *American Journal of Sociology*, LVII (March 1952), 427–442.

31. Alvin W. Gouldner, *Wildcat Strike* (Yellow Springs, Ohio: Antioch Press, 1954).

32. Joseph Bensman and Israel Gerver, "Crime and Punishment in the Factory: The Function of Deviancy in Maintaining the Social System," *American Sociological Review*, XXVIII (August 1963), 588–598.

33. Argyris, *Integrating the Individual and the Organization,* and other writings by the same author. See also the writings of W. F. Whyte; for example, *Patterns of Industrial Peace* (New York: Harper and Row, 1951) and *Money and Motivation* (New York: Harper and Row, 1955)
34. *Ibid.*

3

....

Autonomy and Power:

Limitations to Control

in Complex Organizations

Power is one of the most disagreed-about topics. Every man knows something about power, since every man is both a wielder of some power and a receiver of the effects of other people's power. But few people, including scholars, are able to agree on the nature and substance of power. Thus, even political theory, a field that is greatly concerned with the phenomenon of power, reveals a history of disagreement about the nature of power. John Locke, for example, claimed that power rests with the people but is delegated, with strings attached, to a government. Power, in this case, is not the permanent property of a particular set of persons. It is "traded" as part of the social arrangements that prevail between the citizens of a society and their government. The government must give the people something in exchange, such as order and tranquillity, for its privilege of keeping power. In contrast to Locke, Thomas Hobbes claimed that power necessarily rests with a government because the people, left to their own devices, would bring unspeakable turmoil upon themselves; life would be "nasty, brutish and short." From Hobbes' perspective power must remain with the government.

Among contemporary scholars, disagreement about power is as prevalent as ever. Many sociologists follow the lead of C. Wright Mills and Floyd Hunter in believing power to be located in the hands of a small number of persons who act in unison behind the scenes. The power figures make the important decisions but avoid the limelight; they wield overwhelming influence, in local communities and in the whole country. In contrast to this view, many political scientists are guided by the approach of Robert Dahl, who sees power more nearly in pluralistic terms of pressure groups. Here one finds temporary alliances to cover particular issues. New alliances arise with new issues. Alignments on the new issues are likely to crosscut the alignments on previous issues. Between the two schools there have been heated debates. Disagreement continues.[1]

One of the underlying themes in all the debates is that power must necessarily be limited. If power is used in excess (however one defines "excess"), it will presumably be harmful to the very existence of the society. In Locke's formulation, for example, the assumption is that the power of government must be limited if it is not to become tyrannous. This limitation is accomplished by making the citizenry the ultimate controllers of the government. For Hobbes, on the other hand, the government serves to control the excessive use of power by the citizens and, thereby, reduces the likelihood of tyranny by the people themselves. In the view that sees power wielded by a clique who operate behind the scenes, one can perceive fears about the lack of control over the wielders of power. Thus, in Hunter's *Community Power Structure*[2] there is apprehension about the community's lack of control over the people who are making the community's vital decisions. After all, these people do not run for public office; indeed, they are not likely to be known by many members of the community. There is little to prevent them from acting arbitrarily, even malignantly, toward the community except, possibly, their own self-interest and public-spiritedness. In the pluralistic view, on the other hand, power is seen as a less fearsome phenomenon. Power is thought to be limited by the fact that it is spread out among various groups. Also, the temporariness of any particular alliance of groups tends to lessen the likelihood of excessive power formation. In this view the very form of structuring power tends to produce power limitations.

This book is also concerned with the limits of power. In fact, to say that autonomy is built into social structures is another way of saying that limits to power are structured within social systems. This position should not be taken to mean that structured limits to power exist merely in order to implement the social values that advocate its limitation. A value placed on individual freedom will certainly affect the social relationships in a society. Among other things, such a value is likely to lead to measures to protect the individual members of the society from the encroachments of the government. But the present perspective is broader. It is that there necessarily exist limitations to power in *any* social relationship, be it a relationship that emphasizes individual freedom or the utter subservience of individuals. In the preceding chapters the challenge has been to go beyond this plausible idea and show where, in a particular system, limits to power must exist if that system is to exist. A second challenge is to take a close look at the ways of structuring power itself. How is power incorporated into social roles? How is it blended with other social arrangements?

In Chapter 1 we suggested that if complex organizations are to accomplish their goals, there must be spheres of autonomy—or absence of external control—in the actions of members. Social control itself can be viewed in the same perspective. Our basic proposition is that for any form of social control there exist specifiable forms of autonomy for those who are being controlled. This proposition will be applied to the scheme of compliance in complex organizations developed by Amitai Etzioni. Characteristics of autonomy, which are built into the structure of roles, will be identified for each type of compliance. They will supplement Etzioni's model by clarifying the adaptive and integrative strategies of complex organizations. That is, the distribution of autonomy indicates to what extent outside affiliations are permitted and how tightly members are incorporated into organizations. The organization's "bargain" with its environment becomes revealed. The roots of this approach can be traced to the writings of Max Weber and Bertrand de Jouvenel.

Weber defined control (*Herrschaft*) as "the probability that certain specific commands (or all commands) from a given source will be obeyed by a given group of persons." [3] "It involves a certain minimum of voluntary submission." [4] It is tempting to concentrate on the concepts "submission" and "obedience" set forth in this definition. But do not *probability* of obedience and *voluntary* submission mean that the persons who are subject to authority play an active part in the authority relationship? Does the definition not imply that there remains a sphere of discretion with those who are the subjects of control? If this interpretation is accepted, can one indicate where the spheres of discretion lie for those who are subject to authority? [5]

In his influential work, *On Power*, de Jouvenel expressed apprehension about the enormous power wielded by governments of modern nations. [6] Yet he recognized limitations to power. He noted:

> Obedience has certain limitations within which power must keep. . . . These limits do not remain static throughout the history of a society. For example, the Capetian Kings (who ruled France from 987 to 1328) could not impose direct taxation, and the Bourbons could not exact military service . . .

and

> The fraction or quantum of a society's resources which power can take for its own is theoretically measurable. Clearly it is strictly proportioned to the quantum of obedience . . . [7]

Estimation of the limits of power depends partly on technical measurement procedures. One could, for example, consider the gross national product as a measure of national strength. The proportion of the GNP over which the national government does not exercise control might be considered a measure of the limits of power of the national government. A rough quantitative statement of the national government's power limitation would be:

$$\frac{GNP}{\text{Revenues from taxes}}$$

Measurement procedures are affected by the way in which power is structured in a society. Also, the way power is structured determines the area where power is enacted and the areas where its limitation lies. De Jouvenel sees three ways of structuring power: force, legitimacy, and beneficence.[8] Here the limitations to power would be located, respectively, in the ability to coerce, in the ability to obtain acceptance of the legitimacy of government, and in the acceptance of the government's "credit rating." [9]

Given de Jouvenel and Weber's view of intrinsic limitations to power, can one offer fairly orderly formulations about limitations to power? As a step in this direction, autonomy will be considered as an adjunct to the analysis of complex organizations developed by Etzioni.[10] The objective is not to disparage Etzioni's excellent monograph, but on the contrary, to augment his scheme and, at the same time, illustrate the usefulness of autonomy as a structural concept. Our main concern will not be to test propositions of the Etzioni study, but to strengthen the analytic model.

Etzioni developed a typology of organizations based on whether power is deployed in a coercive, remunerative, or normative way. As corollaries to the forms of power, he postulated for each a kind of compliance—alienative, calculative, or moral involvement in the organization—by "lower participants" [11] within organizations. The results were idealized models. Concrete structures are not apt to be entirely coercive, remunerative, or normative, but the models seem to have enough bearing on concrete reality to make them worthy of serious attention. A scheme of autonomy structure will be applied to each of Etzioni's three analytic types of compliance.

The autonomy scheme contains two dimensions for analyzing the role of participants in organizations. First, how broadly is the participant's organizational role defined: This dimension refers to the number of activities inside the organization for which the organization sets norms; it influences the feasibility of autonomy *external* to an actor's role within the organization. Second, how directly is the role defined? This dimension refers to the degree of detail with which norms specify expected behavior. Do they specify very precisely what the actor should do or do they merely provide guidelines for action? If norms provide precise specifications, then there is little room for autonomy. If they merely provide guidelines, then there is room for autonomy *within* the role, since the actor must interpret the norms. A four-cell scheme is possible.

Table 3. How Roles Are Defined

	DIRECTLY	INDIRECTLY
BROADLY	1	2
NARROWLY	3	4

When one takes an analytic perspective, the four cells appear to offer four clearly different types of roles. When one looks at roles concretely, however, one is apt to find that some types are more viable than others—Etzioni refers to this as "congruence." For instance, it is ordinarily difficult to provide detailed specifications for broadly defined roles, although in principle it is possible. Conversely, direct specification and narrowly defined roles are empirically congruent. And indirect specifications of narrowly defined roles are apt to be troublesome—to actors as well as administrators of organizations.

To illustrate the scheme, the usual sociological conception of the prisoner role can be used, for it is generally considered a precisely defined role that covers virtually all of the inmate's behavior in the prison (Cell 1). It is suggested here that prisoners tend to have two roles. One role consists of submission to official rules in a specific, narrowly defined sphere (Cell 3). The other role consists of *either* submission to detailed rules in a prisoner subculture (a second role in Cell 3) *or* enactment of behavior that is not controlled in detail by prisoner subcultures or official rules, but may take one or both of these as guidelines (Cell 4).

The activities of blue-collar workers in factories typically include a narrow sphere of behavior that is closely specified by rules, especially for those activities involved in technical aspects of work tasks (Cell 3). But there is another sphere where behavior is not closely specified by detailed rules, that of informal patterns of behavior such as those discussed in Chapter 2. When informal worker groups are strongly developed, they may prescribe a broad sphere of the worker's behavior in the factory. This behavior sphere may include detailed rules (Cell 1) or merely strong guidelines to behavior (Cell 2) that are established and enforced by the group.

The behavior of members of a religious congregation or political party is apt to be defined through the use of broad behavioral guidelines, and these tend to cover the total sphere of action of the member's behavior in the organization (Cell 2). Related to broadly defined roles is the fact that a total allegiance to the organization is emphasized and rival allegiances are discouraged. Roles in Cell 2 typify normative commitment. They have autonomy because the behavior is not prescribed in detail; participants need to interpret the rules. But the participants must demonstrate that they are operating within the moral commitment of the organization. There are usually strictures against pursuing drastically different moral alternatives if a member is to remain in good standing.

On the other hand, members of lower ranks in utilitarian organizations can legitimately keep alive alternative allegiances. "Calculative" involvement, typified by roles in Cell 3, includes the right to compare benefits of different organizations while enjoying membership in one organization. The price of this *affiliational* autonomy appears to be limited participation in the host organization. Typically, the factory worker is excluded from policy making and the chief fruits (profits) of the firm for which he works. His informal patterns augment his limited participation in the organization.

In coercive organizations, the participation of low-ranking

members is even more severely curtailed than it is for members of utilitarian organizations. External allegiances are largely severed. But there typically exists a considerable sphere of affiliational autonomy, whether it occurs in the form of uncooperative withdrawal of the mental patient or of the prison subculture that is openly hostile to organizational authorities. In each case alienation is expressed; sometimes it takes the form of well-organized social structures.

Translated into organizational allegiance, the sketches above suggest that in coercive and utilitarian organizations external affiliations are kept alive—legally in utilitarian organizations and illegally in coercive organizations. In normative organizations, external allegiances are minimized. But there exists latitude in participation, provided it can be shown to fall into the sphere of the moral commitment. These characterizations will be elaborated by considering some specific features: prisoner subcultures in relation to coercive organizations, informal groups in relation to utilitarian organizations, and ritual and charisma in relation to normative organizations.

Autonomy Patterns in Coercive Organizations

"Coercion" suggests that a monopoly of power lies in the hands of the wielders of power. Undoubtedly the wielders of power in organizations, such as prisons, concentration camps, and custodial mental hospitals, do in fact have an overwhelming amount of power over the respective groups of inmates. But is it as simple as all that? Can power be wielded with unqualified abandon in these organizations? Studies of coercive organizations suggest that a primordial condition in such organizations is the existence of opposition among inmates toward the "host" organization. Thus Erving Goffman has pointed to tactics and strategies of self-defense among inmates of mental hospitals—tactics that may not constitute open attacks upon the system, but are nevertheless alienative toward the system and intended to lessen the power of those formally charged with the control of the organization.[12] Richard H. McCleery,[13] among others, has pointed to tightly run inmate subcultures that are fundamentally alienative to the prison's formal authority system. But it is hardly satisfactory to say that alienation tends to occur in coercive organizations and leave it at that. What accounts for the presence of alienation? To be sure, one can safely assume that inmates of coercive organizations are frustrated and that this frustration gives rise to alienation. But is this condition sufficient to account for the *continuance* of alienation? In other words, do coercive organizations contain mechanisms for channeling alienation in ways that are relatively harmless, or even useful, to the organization? The answer may lie in the particular way in which "illegitimacy" is permitted to exist.

How does an organization survive and receive a modicum of useful participation by its members if the majority of its members are in the organization against their own will? How does an organization survive if its mission is to incarcerate on a relatively permanent basis persons defined to be socially dangerous? The use of brute coercion—coercion ranging from minor to extreme forms of punishment—immediately comes to mind. But it is unlikely that the continual use of coercive measures is at all feasible or efficient, even if it were approved by the existing morality of the society. The threat of coercion may be a more potent weapon than its exercise, especially when long-term control is needed.

In actual coercive organizations the use of coercive measures tends to be sporadic and infrequent. McCleery, writing about a prison, stated, "A high degree of discipline was maintained with a minimum of direct sanctions." [14] Similar observations have been made about German concentration camps.[15] In short, there appear to be arrangements that rely on the threat of coercion rather than on its continual use. One way of achieving this is to permit an "illegitimate" subculture to exist within the organization. Such a subculture will be under continual threat of disbandment and punishment. But while it exists—which it seems to in many coercive organizations—it may well be useful for both inmates and controllers of the coercive organization. For inmates, the subculture provides a degree of control over their own destiny, "a mechanism for controlling their environment and maintaining self dignity." [16] Usually there is a divergence between the subculture and the administrative culture. Etzioni noted, "[there is] sharp segregation of the 'inmate system' . . . from the rest of the organization. The staff and the inmates are divided into two camps which share few values and mores and have few, if any, social bonds." [17] Such divergence makes it tempting to assume that the administrators derive no benefits from the autonomy of inmates or do not even know of its existence. But these assumptions are questionable. Etzioni's survey suggests that the "inmate elite supports *some* norms in which the guards are interested." [18] McCleery found that much of the mundane, day-to-day control over inmates in an *authorization* prison was virtually delegated by prison authorities to inmate leaders. These leaders supported

> custodial values . . . [with] accent on conformity, on doing one's own time without fear or complaint, on avoiding behavior which would "bring on the heat" . . .
>
> control of a disorganized mass of men was beyond the ability of the guard forces. Control of a rigid social system in which the vast majority of definitions and sanctions were informally imposed [by the prisoner's own leaders] was a far more simple matter. Hence the custodial goals of peace, order and adjustment dictated an alliance between senior officers and inmate leaders . . . in some respects it could be said that the inmates ran the authoritarian prison . . .[19]

During a period of change in the prison, McCleery found that "inmate leaders were . . . able to explain, predict, or control to some degree a situation in which others [prison officials] were helpless and confused." In short, it seems that in the situation described by McCleery the autonomous prisoner subsystem provided distinct benefits for the organization's authorities.

Two more aspects of prison control are relevant. First, the autonomy of inmates is limited. Their system is symbiotic to the rest of the organization rather than completely independent of it; external social status distinctions are severely curtailed and so are contacts with the external world. Inmate social systems, according to McCleery and others, thus appear to be entirely local to the particular organization, rarely tied with ongoing outside structures. Second, emphasis on inmate autonomy must not be allowed to minimize the fact that considerable autonomy still rests with the authorities. In addition to their resources of brute coercive strength, the posture of permitting inmates a "deviant" subsystem forever leaves open the door to a coercive crackdown. Under this perpetual threat the authorities may well be able to drive a hard bargain for a degree of collaboration from the inmate system leaders, as in the situation noted by McCleery.

The preceding formulation relies heavily on one well-known study, namely McCleery's. A more expanded use of studies of coercive organizations might lead to modifications in the model of autonomy in these organizations.

Autonomy Patterns in Utilitarian Organizations

Low-ranking participants in utilitarian organizations have considerably more autonomy within their organizational role than do inmates of coercive organizations. Ordinarily they both join and leave the organization voluntarily. The factory worker and the customer in a store can each terminate his dealings in the respective relationship when he feels dissatisfied and can "take his trade elsewhere." Here, as in the coercive situation, it is necessary to include the participant's autonomy as part of the organizational arrangement. Here, too, one can ask how an organization, or any social relationship, can survive and receive a modicum of cooperation if the participants enjoy autonomy as to whether they will participate. This is especially important when the autonomy is enjoyed not only by those who are in a superordinate position within the relationship but also by those who are clearly in a subordinate position.

The answer to the survival-and-cooperation question for utilitarian organizations appears to lie in the way control and autonomy are balanced, just as it did in coercive organizations. The following model is suggested, based in large measure on the analysis in Chapter 2. The low-ranking participants engage in activities that are narrowly and directly specified by the organization. These activities include the assembly-line worker's activities while he is actually doing his work tasks and the client's activities in selecting and paying for goods in a store. Within this sphere there are precisely stipulated tasks, leaving little room for private judgment. In addition to the directly specified sphere there is another sphere, still among the participant's activities *in* the organization, in which there is considerable autonomy for the participant. The best-known studies on this phenomenon deal with informal groups of workers in factories.[21] The autonomy consists in devising a "way of life," in the work context, that is not controlled by the formal organization.

What has traditionally been called an informal structure of workers is a broad sphere of activity that is controlled by work groups. This structure has been described at length in Chapter 2. The culture of the workingman that is incorporated into the informal structure may actually be drastically different from the norms that govern bureaucratic behavior and may serve to disenfranchise the workingman from bureaucratic advancement. But in exchange for this loss of mobility within the organization, it provides the workingman with continuity with his external way of life in the form of *affiliational* autonomy. This autonomy creates a balance between limited participation in the organization as against the privileges of retaining external loyalties and enacting them within the organization.

Autonomy Patterns in Normative Organizations

Etzioni suggests that the chief basis for compliance in normative organizations is *moral* commitment to the norms of the organization. Rewards are largely symbolic. Normative organizations include religious organizations, many voluntary associations, most political associations, universities, and general hospitals. Some organizations include normative components in conjunction with other forms of control. For example, combat units combine normative and coercive features; most labor unions combine utilitarian with normative features.[22] Finally, although Etzioni deals with "lower" participants rather than elites within organizations, one may hazard the guess that normative allegiance tends to be dominant among the elites in all three types of organization. Etzioni's analysis suggests further that commitment to the organization usually is highest in normative organizations and lowest in coercive organizations.

The first dimension of the corresponding autonomy model is

that moral commitments to an organization constitute guidelines to behavior rather than detailed behavioral prescriptions. This implies that members have autonomy in terms of how they will participate, provided they stay within the guidelines. Second, participation as an organizational member is defined broadly. Affiliation with external organizations is severely curtailed; that is, members have a broad commitment to the organization.

For the organization, the broad commitment of members is achieved at the price of incorporating into the organization continuing threats to its stability and to the direction it pursues. The interpretation of broad norms, which is central to its operating processes, leaves open the possibility of drastic revisions being proposed by the very persons who are staunch adherents to the moral commitment for which the organization stands. To be sure, there are mechanisms for coping with moral deviation, of dealing with persons whose commitment is in doubt. These mechanisms range from harsh treatment toward the open antagonist—the terms "traitor," "heretic," and "apostate" indicate the temper of the response—to the more flexible procedures of cooptation, amalgamation, and collaboration that are used to deal with lesser threats.[23] Another choice is to transfer the harmful person from an influential to a harmless position.[24] There also exist institutional mechanisms, such as ritual, for neutralizing moral zeal. The relevance of ritual deserves some clarification.

One common view of ritual describes it as minutely defined activities which allow little modification and elaboration. But does not ritual in fact permit considerable scope for embellishment by allowing the ritual act to be performed with varying degrees of refinement? Does not the person who performs the ritual act gain stature by displaying virtuosity in his ability to elaborate? In short, is there not autonomy in the enactment of ritual for the sake of demonstrating one's zeal to the moral commitment? A second tradition, the approach of the functional anthropologists, explains ritual in terms of people's efforts to cope with profound uncertainties.[25] Although this explanation may account for the creation of ritual, it is not quite adequate for explaining its persistence as a culture pattern. The persistence can only be explained if ritual has usefulness for the social system in which it occurs. This statement leans on the functional perspective of Emile Durkheim and A. R. Radcliffe-Brown.[26] Radcliffe-Brown's conception of ritual is that it symbolically points to important social conditions and relationships. He said, "the primary basis of ritual . . . is the attribution of ritual value to objects and occasions which are either themselves objects of important common interests linking together the persons of a community or are symbolically representative of such objects." [27] For example, among the Andamans "ritual value is attributed to the cicada, not because it has any social importance itself but because it symbolically represents the seasons of the year which do have importance." But this explanation does not clarify why the important social conditions need to be affirmed. And it does not clarify why they are affirmed at a *particular* time in a *particular* way. Radcliffe-Brown's view stands in opposition to the Malinowskian emphasis on ritual —and magic and religion—as merely meeting psychological needs, especially during crises. Given their antagonism, it is perhaps understandable that the possibility of reconciliation and synthesis of the two views was not recognized by Radcliffe-Brown. The reconciliation seems to lie in seeing that in times of uncertainty and during social transitions it is particularly valuable for the society to have its moral commitments reaffirmed. In addition, ritual can provide personal emotional crutches. Reaffirmation may be necessary because, during crises, the existing commitments are put to a test. Also, such periods may be highly propitious to indoctrination—people "get religion" in times of trouble. Finally, transitional rituals—*rites de passage*—facilitate the learning of new commitments by accentuating the break with preceding commitments. In short, the social system benefits when members of the society can handle their uncertainties. But the particular way of handling uncertainty, by the use of ritual, also reaffirms the moral commitment to the existing way of life. This reaffirmation happens when the Jew blesses the Lord at times of personal bereavement and when the modern Western "ritualistic" bureaucrat takes refuge in administrative rules when he is under pressure.[28] In each of these cases the reaffirmation implies commitment to continue existing arrangements without fundamentally questioning their legitimacy.[29]

It seems that ritual provides a way of expressing moral zeal but, at the same time, the zeal is channeled so that there is minimal interference with existing social structures. It is a way of expressing moral autonomy that is safe and likely to be useful for the social system in which it occurs.

Normative organizations are internally vulnerable since autonomy is an integral part of the legitimate organizational role of members. Norms are forever *legitimately* subject to interpretation. Etzioni noted, "Among the three types of organization [coercive, normative, and utilitarian], 'rebellion' and secession seem to occur most often in normative organizations" [30] and "in normative organizations even deviant leaders tend to come from those who hold organizational [leadership] positions; they rarely emerge directly from the ranks of lower participants." [31] Presumably leaders excel in commitment to the norms. The fervent adherent to the norms is apt to create a following for himself and his interpretation of the norms. He does so while exercising autonomy in the pursuit of the approved moral objectives. The sociology of charisma is relevant here, especially as the presence of charisma acts to blend the autonomy of the leader with the autonomy of followers in normative organizations.

It is customary to think that the influence enjoyed by the charismatic leader is based on his unusual characteristics. To be sure, the charismatic leader is apt to have unusual personal characteristics[32] and to act in relatively independent ways. But to fully explain his influence, it is also necessary to dwell on the characteristics of his followers. He is a leader to whom "sanctity or exemplary character" [33] is attributed. Without *followers-who-attribute* there is no charismatic leadership. The difference between a false prophet and a true prophet may exist in nothing else than the presence or absence of followers who are convinced of the exemplary character of their hero. This situation points to crucial autonomy among followers. Their faith in the leader is a necessary condition to charismatic authority.* Weber emphasized that the

---

* The same applies to Weber's conception of legal and traditional authority. Subjects must believe in the legitimacy of the order for the order to have de facto existence.

charismatic leader must continually prove his powers.[34] But this proof does not make the part played by his followers sufficiently explicit. After all, some of the most elaborate adoration of charismatic persons has occurred after their death. And postmortem adoration may be transformed into important programatic action, such as the establishment of a church. In all these activities there is a vast sphere of innovation by followers. Also, the practices and beliefs of the followers, which constitute the leader's acceptance, may rest on utter misinterpretation of the leader's message. For instance, it has been suggested that "Gandhi never escaped the dilemma that his power was derived from mass beliefs which he considered false." [35]

William H. Friedland has suggested that charisma develops when there is awe, social distance, and deference between followers and leaders.[36] In terms of autonomy one would like to develop a precise, quantitative statement of the *amount* of autonomy—on the part of leaders as well as followers—that is optimal to the development of charismatic leadership. Short of this, one must be satisfied with such qualitative statements as Etzioni's that "the more continuous and closer control elites have over their subordinates, the less likely they are to have charismatic power over them." [37] Close control is apt to inhibit the autonomy of both leaders and followers. The followers are under continuous scrutiny. The leader, on the other hand, "plays his hand," making his intentions and strategy explicitly known to his subjects. He thereby leaves little scope for subjects to invent supreme attributes for the leader.

Summary

Explicitly or implicitly, the need to limit power enters into philosophic treatises on the good society; among present-day students of power the issue still exists, but the debate has taken a new turn. In addition to asking who *ought* to have power and who *ought* to limit the wielders of power, we ask who *does* have power and how *are* the wielders of power limited. We have turned from an analysis of ideals to an analysis of existing social behavior.

The present chapter rests in the ethos of the present. Power is regarded as consisting of socially structured arrangements that must fit in with other existing structures. This theme was explored by analyzing power in particular types of settings, namely, social control in complex organizations. Etzioni's model of normative, coercive, and utilitarian organizations was used to develop corresponding models of configurations of autonomy and control. In each case it was shown that the implementation of power necessarily involves compromises that can be resolved by permitting spheres of autonomy. In other words, control and independence from control together form crucial ingredients in the way social systems reach goals and adapt to their environment.

To be more specific, let us look once again at autonomy in relation to the allegiance of members of organizations. In normative organizations members are expected to have broad allegiance to the organization. But they have autonomy for interpreting the moral guidelines, which means that the potential for disruption is inherent in the approved membership roles. Organizational change is apt to be initiated by those who take the existing norms most seriously and act "for the good of the organization." In coercive organizations, on the other hand, allegiance of low-ranking members is narrowly defined. Autonomy external to the official membership role exists within the organization, although it is officially regarded as illegal and frequently is hostile to the host organization. Opposition is always expected and it can take the form of brute-power confrontations between inmates and organizational authorities. But more commonly there seem to exist tacit arrangements by which each side grants the other a sphere of relatively undisputed autonomy, resulting in peaceful coexistence, at least most of the time. Finally, in utilitarian organizations low-ranking members have limited affiliation with the host organization and are incompletely assimilated into it. They have autonomy to keep alive external affiliations. Their ways of disrupting the organization are by subverting it while ostensibly adhering to its rules. For example, they can restrict output, or they can leave the organization altogether.

Focus on the disruptive potentials of autonomy should not divert attention from the fact that *structuring* autonomy is one of the ways of stabilizing an organization's internal cohesion and adapting it to its social environment.

This chapter is of course exploratory and incomplete. It stresses only one of many possible models of power. Its primary objective has been to show that limitation of power is not merely a topic that excites political philosophers and anyone interested in preserving a particular value system. Limitation of power is also a real component of social structures; it plays a part in the operation of social systems, showing up their strong points and their vulnerabilities.

NOTES ...

1. For a review of the debate, see L. Vaughn Blankenship, "Community Power and Decision-making: A Comparative Evaluation of Measurement Techniques," *Social Forces*, 43, 2 (December 1964), 207–216.

2. Floyd Hunter, *Community Power Structure* (Chapel Hill: University of North Carolina Press, 1953).

3. Max Weber, *The Theory of Social and Economic Organization*, A. M. Henderson and Talcott Parsons, tr. (New York: Free Press, 1947), p. 324.

4. *Ibid.* The translators call *Herrschaft* "imperative control"; Reinhard Bendix translates it as "domination" in his *Max Weber: An Intellectual Portrait* (Garden City, N. Y.: Doubleday, 1960), p. 296.

5. Elliott Jaques used the concept "spheres of discretion" in studies of workers in factories. See Jaques, *Measurement of Responsibility* (Cambridge: Harvard University Press, 1956); and Jaques, *Equitable Payment* (New York: Wiley, 1961). Jaques is chiefly concerned with optimal blending of the individual with the organization in which he works. His "spheres of discretion" are akin to the present ideas about autonomy of those who are the subjects of control.

6. Bertrand de Jouvenel, *On Power: Its Nature and the History of Its Growth*, J. F. Huntington, tr. (Boston: Beacon Press, 1962).

7. *Ibid.*, p. 18. De Jouvenel offers a provisional scheme for measuring power that takes into account limitations to power:

$$\text{Extent of Power} = \frac{\text{the resources at power's disposal}}{\text{the resources inherent in society}}$$

8. *Ibid.*, p. 25.

9. Weber suggested that there exist two types of power; one is based on "a constellation of interests" and one is based on "established authority." Bendix, *Max Weber: An Intellectual Portrait*, p. 294. In the "interest" type of power, limitations to power exist in people's assessment of what their "interests" really are; in the "authority" type, the power is limited by people's part in *granting* legitimacy to the wielder of power.

10. Amitai Etzioni, *A Comparative Analysis of Complex Organizations* (New York: Free Press, 1961). One could have chosen to develop autonomy patterns in relation to other schemes about the nature of power. One could, for instance, have taken Abraham Kaplan's typology of coercion, reward, personal loyalties, sense of legitimacy and expertness as the point of departure. See Kaplan, "Power in Perspective," *Power and Conflict in Organizations*, Robert L. Kahn and Elise Boulding, eds. (New York: Basic Books, 1964). However, Etzioni seems to offer the most completely developed scheme and, therefore, the most inviting formulation.

11. Etzioni, *ibid.*, p. 5, 16 ff.

12. Erving Goffman, *Asylums* (Chicago: Aldine, 1961).

13. Richard H. McCleery, "Policy Change in Prison Management," *Complex Organizations: A Sociological Reader*, Amitai Etzioni, ed. (New York: Holt, Rinehart and Winston, 1961).

14. *Ibid.*, p. 381.

15. See, for example, Bruno Bettelheim, *The Informed Heart* (New York: Free Press, 1960).

16. Gresham M. Sykes and Sheldon L. Messinger, "The Inmate Social System," *Theoretical Studies in Social Organization of the Prison* (Social Science Research Council, Pamphlet 15, 1960). Cited by Charles R. Tittle and Drollene P. Tittle, "Social Organization of Prisoners: An Empirical Test," *Social Forces* 43, 4 (October 1964) 216–222.

17. Etzioni, *A Comparative Analysis of Complex Organizations*, p. 96.

18. *Ibid.*, p. 97

19. McCleery, "Policy Change in Prison Management," p. 385.

20. *Ibid.*, p. 384.

21. The Western Electric studies are the most famous example. See F. J. Roethlisberger and W. J. Dickson, *Management and the Worker* (Cambridge: Harvard University Press, 1939).

22. Etzioni, *A Comparative Analysis of Complex Organizations*, Chap. II.

23. *Ibid.*, pp. 103 ff.

24. Phillip E. Hammond and Robert E. Mitchell, "Segmentation of Radicalism—The Case of the Protestant Campus Minister," *American Journal of Sociology*, LXXI, 2 (September 1965), 133–143.

25. See Bronislaw Malinowski, *Magic, Science and Religion* (New York: Free Press, 1948); also Raymond Firth, *Elements of Social Organization* (Boston: Beacon Press, 1963), Chap. VII. A. R. Radcliffe-Brown raises the question whether ritual may not *induce* fear and uncertainty; see his book *Structure and Function in Primitive Society* (London: Cohen and West, 1952), pp. 148–149.

26. See Radcliffe-Brown, *Structure and Function in Primitive Society*, Chap. VII.

27. *Ibid.*, p. 151.

28. Robert K. Merton, *Social Theory and Social Structure*, rev. ed. (New York: Free Press, 1957), pp. 149–153, 184–187.

29. This perspective points to articulation of personality with existing social structures. For a similar viewpoint, see Melford E. Spiro, "An Overview and Suggested Reorientation," *Psychological Anthropology: Approaches to Culture and Personality*, F. L. K. Hsu, ed. (Homewood, Ill.: Dorsey Press, 1961), pp. 459–492.

30. Etzioni, *A Comparative Analysis of Complex Organizations*, p. 105.

31. *Ibid.*

32. Weber said, "The term 'Charisma' will be applied to a certain quality of an individual personality by virtue of which he is set apart from ordinary men and treated as endowed with supernatural, superhuman, or at least specifically exceptional power or qualities. These are such as are not accessible to the ordinary person, but are regarded as of divine origin or as exemplary, and on the basis of them the individual concerned is treated as a leader." (Weber, *The Theory of Social and Economic Organization*, pp. 358–359.)

33. Bendix, *Max Weber: An Intellectual Portrait*, p. 413.

34. Weber, *The Theory of Social and Economic Organization*, p. 360.

35. Reinhard Bendix, *Nation-Building and Citizenship: Studies of Our Changing Social Order* (New York: Wiley, 1964), p. 242.

36. See William H. Friedland, "For a Sociological Concept of Charisma," *Social Forces*, XLIII, 1 (October 1964), 18–26. Friedland noted that, psychologically speaking, potentially charismatic persons probably exist quite frequently. But the social context that is conducive to their acceptance as charismatic leaders needs to be analyzed. In his study of change in Tanganyika he suggested that charisma emerged when leaders formulated inchoate sentiments held by the masses, when the expression of such sentiments was dangerous, and when there was some success as defined by the relevant groups.

37. Etzioni, *A Comparative Analysis of Complex Organizations*, p. 213.

part ii   A FIELD STUDY OF AUTONOMY
AMONG PROFESSIONALS

4

....

The Case of

Medical Pathologists:

An Overview

This is a study of the autonomy of some members of one profession. It does not claim to be statistically representative of all members of that profession. It does not try to study everything about any of the members. It does attempt to see how solutions are worked out to some problems and issues that all professionals and administrators of complex organizations must face and how autonomy plays a part in these solutions. Basically the problems are those of the highly specialized professional in the modern society. Which arrangements will assure that his contributions are effectively developed and used by others while, at the same time, leaving him with a necessary and viable independence? The days of the independent professional are on the wane. Increasingly the professional must be attuned to a large social organization or, at least, to a large number of fellow specialists. He must find ways of adapting to complex social interactions.

We shall focus on a particular group of physicians, those who perform tissue examinations, autopsies, and clinical laboratory tests. This necessarily means that the issues discussed will be formulated around problems of medical practice. But the issues are fundamentally similar to those faced by other professions. It is not the uniqueness of the medical profession but its similarity to other professions that gives it sociological interest.

Three broad assumptions underlie this study of pathologists. First, in order for professionals and their clients to have transactions, each must have spheres of autonomy. Thus professionals must have a sphere of discretion in which to exercise their professional judgment and clients must be protected from being victimized by professionals. Typically the client is in a disadvantaged position. He comes to the professional with a problem and the professional has more knowledge about solutions to his problem than he does. The client's autonomy consists in being able to terminate his reliance on one professional and switching to another professional or, at least, getting corroboration from another professional. But there is another dimension to the part autonomy plays in the relationship. The client benefits from the professional's autonomy and the professional benefits from the client's autonomy. The fact that the professional has room to maneuver in his field of knowledge is conducive to the development of expertise and, therefore, promises help for the client. On the other hand, the professional is protected by the client's autonomy. For example, the lawyer can defend the murderer with zeal and dedication without being accused of approving murder or somehow being in personal league with the murderer. Similarly the physician can treat an immoral patient with dedication and skill without running the risk of being accused of sharing the patient's immorality.

The second assumption is that guarantees of autonomy are incorporated into the professional's work arrangements. Increasingly, professionals are found working in large bureaucratic organizations. The assumption here is that each type of arrangement incorporates *fairly definite prerogatives for professional autonomy into a fairly stable set of social relationships.* A basic objective of the present study is to compare different arrangements in order to see where autonomy lies and to try to assess the benefits and the price that is paid for this autonomy by the participants.

The third assumption is that work arrangements of professionals are linked to the status struggles of these professionals. Pathologists, for example, seek to be paid fees rather than salaries in order to gain a status that is comparable to that of clinicians. From this point of view, one can regard the work arrangements of professionals as attempts to solve the profession's status problems. But a profession is apt to have a variety of status problems. And work arrangements are apt to include a variety of social arrangements. Hence work arrangements are apt to be sets of solutions to sets of problems. The solutions are likely to give high priority to some problems and low priority to others. In addition, the solutions are likely to involve compromises toward the existing local environment. These processes suggest a fairly chaotic picture. To discover some order within them, an attempt will be made to show the areas of autonomy and areas of subservience to external control that exist in the different work arrangements.

The first stage of the study of pathologists was a comprehensive survey of medical writings. This survey yielded a report on the historical development of pathology as a medical specialty in the United States and an analysis of contemporary status characteristics of pathologists. It showed that pathologists have moved from a pure-science orientation toward a search for increased participation in clinical medicine.[1] This shift has given rise to various problems in pathologists' dealings with clinicians and hospital administrators. In the second stage of the study three different types of practice arrangements were examined in detail.[2] All the pathologists of one state were interviewed. Three pathologists were singled out for intensive case study. The following discussion is based largely on the findings from these three cases.

There is every indication that the practice for each of the three pathologists is a coherent structure that includes both work arrangements and an ethic that accompanies these arrangements. The ethic is made up of beliefs about professional responsibilities and conceptions of what is and what is not professional medical activity. The concern here is not whether the ethic or the work arrangement came first, but merely that they existed together at the time of the study.

Each complex, made up of work arrangement and ethic, can be thought of as a set of adaptations to the pathologist's professional problems. It includes "answers" to the question of what constitutes the practice of medicine for pathologists. The answers differ for each of the three working-arrangement relationships. One can think of each complex as a form of social anchorage. Each has different roots and, indeed, each seeks to put its roots in different soil. In terms of the structure of autonomy, each complex contains distinctive areas of autonomy and distinctive exchange processes—autonomy is gained in one sphere and external control is accepted in another. Finally, external control appears, in each complex, to be accepted only on the contingent basis that clearly defined areas of autonomy are reserved for those who accept the controls. The descriptions that follow attempt to describe the full concrete reality in which the pathologist works while, at the same time, preserving the necessary degree of attention to the importance of autonomy.

The study, as we said, began with an intensive survey of the medical literature dealing with the historical development of pathology as well as the contemporary problems of the profession's distinctive identity and adaptation to the work conditions in hospitals.[3] The second part of the study was based on direct observation and interviews with pathologists as they went about their day-to-day activities.[4] These observations were supplemented by interviews with other physicians and hospital administrators. The individual pathologists were chosen because they demonstrated different ways of organizing the practice of pathology. The choices were made on the basis of the various administrative arrangements that became evident in the first study. We decided to pick a pathologist who was in independent practice, a pathologist who had a fee or percentage arrangement, and a pathologist who had a salary arrangement with a hospital.

In independent practice the physician owns and operates a laboratory service, either as a concession in a hospital or in quarters altogether separate from any hospital. He employs personnel, such as technicians and secretaries, to help him. He is essentially an entrepreneur: he does his own billing of patients, assumes risks of loss from nonpayment of bills, and otherwise shares in the "business side" of private enterprise. He may or may not have contractual arrangements with hospitals to do all or part of their pathology work. In technical matters he is governed largely by his own resourcefulness and the economic means at his disposal. This implies, for example, that he enjoys greater freedom in the choice of procedures than his hospital-affiliated colleagues, who depend, at least to some extent, upon existing hospital regulations.

The arrangement that is increasingly popular with pathologists is the one where they either receive a fee for each professional service or a percentage of the income accruing to the laboratory.* Under the fee arrangement the pathologist charges for each professional service he renders, and the hospital's bill to the patient usually indicates that a portion of the total professional fee goes to the pathologist. In this system there arise questions as to what constitutes a "professional service" by the pathologist. There is little doubt that reading and interpreting a tissue slide is regarded as a professional service, but there is some question as to whether the supervision of clinical tests is a professional service since the pathologist takes little part in the day-to-day routine of doing the tests. Under the percentage arrangement the pathologist receives a fixed proportion of the income from the laboratory as his professional "fee." The percentage and fee arrangements are similar. In the latter a fee is usually charged for clinical laboratory-test supervision as well as for tissue diagnoses. The billing is usually done by the hospital, but a professional fee for the pathologist is included and is indicated as such. In the present study the pathologist has a fee arrangement. Tissue and clinical services are combined, but the bulk of the income comes from the latter since the number of clinical tests performed in the course of a day is very large.

The salary method is the oldest form of arrangement between the pathologist and his hospital. The pathologist is considered an employee of the hospital and occupies the rank of department chief. In the past this has frequently meant a relatively low status for the pathologist; he might be ranked on a par with the chief

---

* Data on the exact proportion of persons under these arrangements are not available.

of the housekeeping department rather than with the chief of surgery. Since World War II, the status of pathologists, including that of the salaried pathologist, has improved considerably. Nonetheless, the phrase "employee of the hospital" is hardly a term of approbation to many pathologists. There have been efforts to declare salary arrangements to be the "illegal practice of medicine by the hospital." Hospital administrators have resented and resisted these efforts. To the administrator the pathologist's status aspirations frequently represent interference with the administrator's authority over the laboratory's income and an "unrealistic" view of the hospital's primary mission.[5] All the pathologists who were interviewed for the present study, including those on salary arrangement, expressed the view that the salaried pathologist in private (i.e., nongovernment) hospitals was becoming a phenomenon of the past.

Our historical survey showed that pathology is a medical specialty that in some ways—such as its lack of direct doctor-patient relationships—is removed from the core of medical practice as it has traditionally been viewed by both the public and the medical profession itself. This specialty was once regarded as the very kernel of the "science," as contrasted with the "practice," of medicine. Recent developments, however, have eroded pathology's key position. Witness its two principal areas: clinical pathology is in part being parceled out to other specialties, and tissue pathology has taken a somewhat secondary place relative to more modern developments in medicine.* Pathologists have become aware of the threat to their specialty, especially as manifested by the difficulty of recruiting new physicians for it. Although their numbers have increased they believe they are attracting disproportionately few of these young physicians.

The pathologist has adapted to this situation by attempting to gain acceptance in a clinician-type role. The clinician differs from the pathologist in that he has direct contact with patients

* Clinical pathology consists of the various laboratory tests—chemical, biochemical, hematological, and serological—that are used to diagnose disease as well as to check the course of a disease and its treatment. Most of these tests are carried out by a staff of technicians under the supervision of a chief technician who, in turn, is responsible to the pathologist. The latter has, in most hospitals, overall charge of the laboratories. Tissue pathology consists of the gross and microscopic examination of the body tissue, including the performance of autopsies.

for whom he has primary responsibility and who constitute his clientele. This is not meant to suggest that all patients enter the hospital as patients of particular clinicians or that a hospitalized patient can have only one physician who regards him as "his patient." Yet the fact remains that the pathologist does not have a patient clientele who come to the hospital as his patients, whereas the clinician does. In his relationships with the hospital's administration the clinician is, therefore, more nearly an independent agent than the pathologist. The pathologist's efforts toward getting a role similar to that of the clinician include an educational campaign within the medical profession to make room for the pathologist at the bedside and a drive to get the same employment arrangement within the hospitals that clinicians enjoy. Hospital administrators view these efforts as disruptive and dysfunctional to the hospital. In the view of the administrators, pathologists are more nearly heads of service departments than independent practitioners. They apparently do not comprehend the urgency of the role aspirations that motivate pathologists.

The tactics and strategy adopted by pathologists are almost identical with those of the specialties of anesthesiology, radiology, and physical medicine. The four specialties have, on occasion, banded together in bringing legal suits against hospitals in order to win a "fee basis." The only sociological study available on these specialties is one on anesthesiology.[6] This study shows what probably applies to physical medicine and radiology as well—that anesthesiologists are attempting to gain acceptance for their relatively new specialty as a full-fledged medical specialty. They claim that they should have major responsibility for the patient during operations and that they should see patients prior to operations. In short, they desire a "sphere" of the patient—much as pathologists do. Anesthesiology, radiology, and physical medicine are, in contrast to pathology, relatively new specialties. All four share the characteristics of the absence of primary responsibility for the patient. The efforts of these specialists may be seen as part of the problems created by the rapid increase in specialties and specialtsts.[7] The problems center around the allocation of responsibility for the patient, the delineation of the spheres of the various medical specialties, and the integration of the role aspirations of the different specialties with the needs of hospitals as complex organizations that have relatively specific goals.

The pathologist's job in the hospital involves him in a wide range of activities, which cast him in a number of distinctly different roles. Among these roles are (1) "Policeman" (In the course of examining surgically removed tissue or performing autopsies, the pathologist may uncover mistakes made by other doctors. His subsequent course of action may involve his acting as "policeman"); (2) Department head (The administration of the laboratory includes directing a staff of technicians); (3) "Teacher" (Not only is the pathologist expected to "teach" the medical staff what laboratory facilities are available, and what the laboratory can and cannot do, but he is usually assigned a prominent part in case conference on disease processes); and (4) Researcher and scientist (Pathologists have a tradition of engaging in research work on disease processes).

It will be apparent at once that each of these roles can involve the pathologist in conflict situations. The role of policeman, for example, may involve the pathologist in disputes with surgeons over "unnecessary" surgery. In addition to factors inherent in the particular roles, the pathologist must make some reconciliation between the duties involved in his different roles. For example, as administrator of the laboratory he may be torn between aiding his technicians in disputes with clinicians and siding with his medical colleagues.[8] All of these features were detailed in the analysis of the medical literature.[9]

NOTES ...

1. Fred E. Katz, "Pathologists, a Sociological Study of the Professional Relationships of a Medical Specialty" (Master's thesis, University of North Carolina, 1956).

2. Fred E. Katz, "The Profession of Pathology: a Sociological Study of Patterning in Medical Practice" (Doctoral dissertation, University of North Carolina, 1961).

3. Katz, "Pathologists, a Sociological Study."

4. For a detailed review of the research methods and findings, see Katz, "The Profession of Pathology."

5. Katz, "Pathologists, a Sociological Study," pp. 99–103.

6. Dan C. Lortie, "Doctors without Patients: The Anesthesiologist, a New Medical Specialty" (Master's thesis, University of Chicago, 1950)

7. See W. T. Fitts and B. Fitts, "Ethical Standards of the Medical Profession," Bulletin of the American College of Surgeons, XLI (January–February 1956), 23 ff. These authors note that the number of specialists certified by boards has increased from 16,000 in 1940 to 52,000 in 1953, or one third of all practicing physicians. Since that time the rapid increase of specialists has continued.

8. On the basis of this dual orientation of the laboratory chief and the influence of both physicians and hospital administrative personnel, the laboratory has been described as a "hybrid" department. See H. L. Smith, "Two Lines of Authority," The Modern Hospital, LXXXIV (March 1950), 59–64.

9. Katz, "Pathologists, a Sociological Study."

5

....

Autonomy in Adapting to Administrative Controls

Pathologists, being specialized professionals, have definite technical professional skills. Their professional functions also involve administrative and business factors, such as record keeping, billing services, ownership of equipment, as well as personnel responsibilities concerning laboratory technicians. If the business and administrative tasks are performed by the pathologist, this means that the pathologist has a larger area of responsibility than he has traditionally been granted. If this new according of responsibility is to work, it must be accepted by those with whom the pathologist has dealings. Typically the administration-minded pathologist must find a way of seeing "medical" legitimacy for doing administrative work; he must also find some way of enforcing this conception by incorporating it into his work arrangements. If the administrative tasks are accomplished by a separate agency, notably the hospital, there arise problems around safeguarding the pathologist's professional autonomy from outside administrative encroachment. When the pathologist is his own administrator, his professional autonomy is also threatened. The threat comes from the expansive definition of his role—his internal role autonomy. In both cases the issue revolves around the problem of separating the professional sphere from the administrative sphere. The issue is solved differently in each of the salaried, fee-based, and entrepreneurial types of practice.

Administrative Control—Professional Autonomy

In the survey it was found that pathologists perceive infringements on their professional domain by what they feel are excessive administrative controls by hospitals. Conversely, hospital administrators perceive pathologists to be rebellious in areas they feel they must exercise control, such as limiting expenditures for equipment. The issue is that many of the pathologist's tasks include considerations of economy and business efficiency, which are largely under the guardianship of hospital administrators, as well as considerations of professional independence by the physician. Identification of different forms of adaptation to administrative control by pathologists is, therefore, highly pertinent.

Doubtless the most complete abrogation of administrative control by hospital administrators is achieved by the entrepreneur pathologist, for he is his own administrator. He sets his own rates, employs his own staff, and owns his equipment. In the words of the entrepreneurial pathologist, this control "gives [him] a freedom which other pathologists do not have." He has, in his view, maximized professional autonomy by incorporating into his "professional" domain broad administrative functions.

The practice of the salaried and fee-based pathologist represents ipso facto acceptance of the legitimacy of a degree of control by the hospital administration over the professional domain of the pathologist. The bases for this acceptance are worth examining. Sociologists since the time of Max Weber have been attuned to the contingent and, often, diverse motives for obedience to authority.[1] In the present situation, obedience to control results from the pathologists' confidence that the administrator shares certain core values with the pathologist* and that the administrator is basically competent. It is based, also, on the fact that they receive certain guarantees of recognition for their professional status. But the guarantees for the two types of pathologists differ in emphasis and in the manner in which they are structured.

In the situation of the fee-based pathologist, the matter of being recognized as an independent professional is essentially *built into* the formal arrangement with the hospital. He has an agreement with the hospital whereby he receives a "professional share" of all the income accruing to the laboratory. His share is indicated on the patient's bill. Thus he has achieved a major status symbol of the physician who practices in hospitals. But recognition of the pathologist's stature was not easily obtained. The opposition came from clinicians who resented the degree of autonomy granted to the pathologist. The administration of the hospital, especially the chairman of the trustees, acted to curb the encroachments by powerful clinicians upon what the pathologist considered his own domain. The pathologist was thereby granted protection of his professional autonomy.

An incident related by the fee-based pathologist will illustrate this statement. He is the first full-time pathologist at his hospital. Previously a pathologist had served on a part-time basis, and in addition, some material was sent to other hospitals for analysis. When the present pathologist was approached about taking a position at the hospital, he had just completed his residency. During the initial interview with the chairman of the trustees, the pathologist remarked that "many a young pathologist has been sacrificed because an old surgeon has complained to the chairman of the trustees, and the pathologist is kicked out!" Within six months after the pathologist's arrival at the hospital the prediction was almost fulfilled. The surgeon "with the worst record for improper surgery" complained to the chairman of the trustees

* The salaried pathologist stated that he "is confident" that the administrator's primary goal was "the good of the hospital." He agreed, also, with the administrator's evaluation of the desire of pathologists and kindred specialists to declare unethical the "salary basis" of employment arrangement. He said, "[The administrator] said, 'They call it ethics, but really they want more money for themselves' . . . and he's right." Similarly, the pathologist on the fee basis expressed an affinity for the values of the administrator and chairman of the trustees of his hospital.

about the pathologist. The surgeon was an elderly, well-established man; the pathologist was a young man, just beginning his career. The chairman of the trustees told the surgeon, said the pathologist, "how I was here to do a job, and doing a good job." The surgeon has since left the hospital. The hospital's chief administrative officer has thus helped define and guarantee the role of the pathologist in a manner that indicates a degree of professional autonomy and a status that is not subservient to that of the established surgeons.

On the other hand, the professional recognition accorded to the salaried pathologist involves attempts on the part of the administrator to free the pathologist from purely routine administrative work so that he may pursue independent scientific interests. Also, the administrator has attempted to lessen the pathologist's immediate dependence on administrative control. Statements by the administrator illustrate these points:

> I have been after him to get equipment and assistants, so that he would have more time for pathology and [would need to spend] less time on purely administrative work . . . his chief interest is scientific

> A professional man is bound to hate to have to beg for equipment and assistants from the administrator . . . I try to avoid the need for this . . . [I] would feel the same way if I were a professional man.

The administrator's effort to provide professional recognition for the salaried pathologist is at odds with the stereotyped view of the salaried pathologist as being one step removed from nonmedical employees of the hospital. This strong support for the pathologist appears to underlie the salaried pathologist's statements that his work situation in the hospital is "almost ideal." The administrator's statements suggest, however, that the pathologist depends considerably upon the continuing good will of the administrator. The suggestion is further confirmed by the salaried pathologist's explicit deference and subservience to his hospital administrator. The pathologist says that the administrator "rules with an iron hand . . . [he] gives me hell, but only when I deserve it." In contrast with this relationship, there is the fee-based pathologist's report of egalitarian dealings with the administrator and chairman of the board of trustees of his hospital.

In both situations there is indication that the pathologists receive substantial facilities for doing professional work. The salaried pathologist states, "I can get along with our administrator . . . this enables me to get what I think I need" and "He gives me good laboratory equipment . . . even though it costs him money." The fee-based pathologist remarks that at his hospital "Doctors get more of the things they want than at any other hospital I know of" and ". . . I am here to do a good job. That's why I can go to [the chairman of the trustees] and say, 'I need a thousand-dollar microscope,' and he'll give it to me." In each situation, then, there is little doubt that control rests with the hospital administration. But it is evident, also, that the pathologists perceive a degree of deference to their needs as professionals.

These examples show the justification involved in the acceptance of administrative authority. They are in keeping with the formulations by Weber concerning the contingent nature of the acceptance of the "rational-legal" form of authority.[2] In large part, the justification for acceptance of administrative control by both the salaried and fee-based pathologists was that their professional needs were being met adequately. Thus, even in the situation where there is minimal formal guarantee of professional autonomy in the structure of the pathologist's hospital arrangement, there exists a mutually agreeable solution. Specifically, the pathologist's acceptance of administrative authority and the administrator's deference to professional needs comprise this additional dimension to the formal structure of their respective situations. The organizational structure, it is evident, permits a degree of flexibility by individuals that can guarantee protection of vital professional interests. (Of course, the opposite could happen: The flexibility could be used to infringe upon the professional domain.) Hence, while the fee-based and salaried pathologists do not enjoy formally structured freedom from administrative control to the extent that the entrepreneur does, they do in fact enjoy sufficient professional freedom to satisfy themselves. To be sure, their autonomy is heavily affected by their relationship to their particular administrator; the arrival of a new administrator might completely alter their situation. On the other hand, they enjoy professional autonomy while having minimal administrative responsibilities. The entrepreneur, by contrast, has heavy administrative responsibilities along with his more formally guarded professional autonomy. He is largely "free" of administrative control by hospitals; his salaried and fee-based colleagues are largely "free" of administrative duties.

The Laboratory: Professional Sphere—Administrative Sphere

A traditional view depicts the pathologist as unconcerned about the affairs and administrative matters of the hospital, contented to remain in his "backroom," interested only in his tissue slides and work in the morgue. But since World War II there has been a greatly heightened concern by pathologists with their professional status—their standing among medical specialties and their recognition in the hospital.[3] This concern has been accompanied by broader participation in hospital affairs and processes of redefining and widening the pathologist's professional sphere of work. These efforts involve actual or potential conflict between hospital administrators and pathologists about which services constitute legitimate *professional* services and the manner in which the income from disputed services is to be utilized.

The area of contention centers largely around clinical laboratory services. The salaried pathologist is essentially in the position of the traditional pathologist who is "administratively" employed to run the laboratory. That is, the clinical laboratory services are essentially regarded as hospital services under the domain of the administration. Conversely, the fee-based and entrepreneurial pathologists regard clinical services as primarily professional services, which they supervise professionally and for which they are entitled to professional fees. Before examining the adaptations involved in these working structures, it is necessary to summarize the findings of the previous study about the nature of the conflict between administrators and pathologists concerning laboratories.

The bulk of the work—"running the tests"—is performed by technicians, who are usually supervised by a chief technician.[4] Over them, in turn, is the pathologist who has overall responsibility. In actuality, he is consulted when unusual results occur but may have little immediate contact with the bulk of the work that is performed. Laboratory services are playing an expanding part in medical work, and the income accruing from these services is considerable. The debate over the management of this income arises partly from the very magnitude of the funds involved and partly from differences of definition as to the nature of the services rendered. Concerning the latter, it was said:

> A laboratory test may be regarded by a clinician as a service to himself in his treatment of a patient. The pathologist may regard it as the "practice of medicine," and the hospital administrator may regard the same test as one of the "hospital services" performed by a department of the hospital.[5]

Pathologists' associations have been working for recognition of the various laboratory services as professional medical services. For some of these services, such as morphological tissue examination, the professional designation has long been accepted. But other services, such as blood tests and urinalyses, are still frequently considered routine hospital services rather than professional services. Pathologists have attempted to remove the laboratory from the domain of hospital services and bring it more closely into the sphere of professional services.

Concerning the utilization of the income from laboratories, the disagreement was summarized as follows:

> The administrator's point of view is: "The laboratory is part of the entire organization and the surplus income is used to offset deficits in operating units that have expenses but no or little independent income." Pathologists hold that the proceeds from the laboratory are the product of their professional services and that the hospital is, therefore, profiting from their professional services—a situation which medical associations have termed unethical.[6]

Pathologists hold that their professional status is vitally involved in this issue. Administrators, on the other hand, tend to interpret pathologists' demands as the quest for more and more money at the expense of administrative efficiency and control.

Accommodations to problems of administrative versus professional control over the laboratory can be illustrated from the hospital of the salaried pathologist. Although the pathologist is satisfied with his salary arrangement, he advocates that the allocation of the income from laboratory services be "professionally indicated." The administrator, in the same conciliatory way, reports that he regards pathologists' recent endeavors to greater professional status as motivated primarily by a desire to increase his income; yet he sends the pathologist a monthly statement showing the laboratory's income because "he's entitled to know this."

In this situation there is mutual accommodation and awareness of conditions under which the other party operates. The salaried pathologist reports that he has doubts as to the "medical" character of some laboratory activities. He states, "a good deal of what goes on in this laboratory, of course it's all supposed to be under my direction, but I have a hard time viewing some of it as the practice of medicine." He agrees with the administrator that some of the "professional" demands of his fellow pathologists may really be a guise for a desire for a larger income. The administrator, on the other hand, notes that he needs to help safeguard the professional status of the pathologist; for example, the pathologist should not have to "beg the administrator" for laboratory equipment. Here one sees mutually complementary attitudes. Each gives credence to the other and, indeed, does some championing of the other's needs. Each is offering some autonomy to the other.

The pathologist believes that a portion of the laboratory's income should be used to employ more professionally trained persons in the laboratory. The necessity for this arises, according to the pathologist, from the need for closer professional supervision of technicians. He states:

> I am concerned about getting my people to do their best work; I feel guilty when I feel they don't . . . We have a fair number of inexperienced people. They need the experience and they make mistakes. I hear about some of them, but there are some that nobody hears about.

He regards the use of some laboratory funds for this purpose as "professionally necessary." An indication of the rapprochement between the pathologist and the administrator is the fact that toward the end of the research phase of the study, the pathologist's goals were implemented: Two additional physicians—a biochemistry specialist and a pathologist—were added to the laboratory's staff. Similarly, the pathologist helped increase the income accruing to the laboratory by revising the schedule of charges for laboratory tests after making a systematic study of the charges made by other laboratories. This schedule was approved and adopted by the administrator. In this situation it appears that the pathologist recognizes the financial pressures under which the administrator operates. In turn, the administrator respects the professional orientations of the pathologist. Resulting accommodations by both sides have given the laboratory a broadened professional base without significantly diminishing the influence or revenue of the administrative sphere.

In the situation of the fee-based pathologist, on the other hand, one sees acceptance of pathologists' desire to have the laboratory recognized as a distinctly professional sphere with the pathologist as its chief. All laboratory services, clinical tests as well as tissue diagnoses, include a "professional factor" as part of the charge that accrues to the pathologist. A concomitant of this is that the pathologist is more nearly in "private practice" than his salaried colleague. Thus he assumes a degree of risk as to the size of his income, whereas the salaried pathologist receives a guaranteed income. An indication of this difference is the fee-based pathologist's attunement to *decreases* in volume of work, whereas the salaried pathologist is likely to be attuned chiefly to *increases* in work load. (It was a fee-based pathologist who reported that there was a lessened volume of work and lessened income during the summer months. He attributed the slackening to the fact that the hospital was not air-conditioned, so that patients came to the hospital only for dire emergencies.)

Another concomitant of the fee-based pathologist's dominant status in the laboratory is that the laboratory is virtually a self-contained unit. The hospital administration's minimal participation must be matched by increased managerial duties on the part of the pathologist. These duties include, preeminently, the preservation of employee morale and settling "interpersonal problems," in addition to the technical professional tasks of supervision. The fee-based pathologist stated, "keeping everyone happy is one of my major tasks" and "when they go on vacation I give them twenty or thirty dollars spending money; when they are out for a day I tell them how we missed them." In short, it seems that the pathologist, in obtaining the enhanced prestige and authority that accompany an expanded professional sphere, has inherited new administrative functions that are somewhat different from those of the traditional technical specialist. In this respect he resembles the entrepreneur—both have acquired administrative functions beyond the core of their medical specialization.

Technical Expert—Administrative Expert

Our historical survey suggested that pathologists were participants in the "silent warfare" of technical experts against administrative experts in hospitals.[7] A major characteristic of the technical expert was his lack of business attributes, such as ownership of equipment and participation in billing patients. Much of the disagreement between administrators and pathologists revolved around pathologists' attempts to acquire business attributes in a quest for recognition of their status as full-fledged medical practitioners.

In the three arrangements under review, the entrepreneur participates most fully in business activities and the salaried pathologist participates least. The entrepreneur owns his own laboratory equipment and sends bills to patients. The fee-based pathologist does not himself send a bill to patients, but he receives a specific payment from patients. The salaried pathologist receives payment only from the hospital. Neither the salaried nor fee-based pathologist owns the laboratory equipment. The salaried pathologist is essentially the purest professional pathologist in the sense of adhering only to the substantive technical features of the specialty. The entrepreneur, because he is not a member of a bureaucratic organization, must perform a variety of administrative tasks. His problem is to create professional legitimacy and prestige for those business activities that have traditionally been separate from the pathologist's functions, having been performed by the hospital administration. The entrepreneur and the salaried pathologists are virtually at opposite poles in these respects. It is, therefore, appropriate to compare their views, especially as they relate to their respective structural settings.

The salaried pathologist gave primacy to the role of "technical specialist" and was prepared to relinquish the "business" or administrative aspects to the hospital management. He believed that it was an advantage to be free of the need to deal with the lay public. He also expressed gratification at not having to be concerned with collecting payment for overdue bills. (He receives a fixed salary and is not affected by losses incurred from failure of patients to pay their bills.) He is happy that he does not have to appease lay people, saying, "I don't have to answer a lot of silly questions and back talk [from families of patients]." He also said:

> We [in the laboratory] make money and the hospital uses some of it for other purposes, and this is troublesome in some areas. There is a way the administration has of not letting us know the actual cost of various procedures. But this doesn't bother me the way it seems to worry some people. I know there are some departments, such as the laundry service, which have no income and render us services . . .

These statements indicate willingness to accept a minor part in the disposal of income in return for a degree of protection and shielding from participation in business transactions with the general public. Stated more positively, his organizational arrangement was a way of implementing his preference for isolation from the general public and concentration on the technical content of his professional role.

It must be pointed out that the salaried pathologist was by no means aloof from the affairs of the hospital. But his participation centered around adjuncts to technical medical matters. For example, he served as the adviser to medical residents, he had been chief of service for the medical staff, and he performed all the medical photography. He also promoted the laboratory technician-training program, concerning himself with recruitment, admissions procedures, and the procurement of funds for the program. But here, again, the training of substantive experts was the purpose.

The entrepreneur adopted the view that participation in business matters by the physician had professional and medical legitimacy. He implied by this view that attention to business matters is an essential part of private practice. It is necessary, that is, to assess accurately "where the money goes"; and, further, a concern with "good business" methods does not preclude professional excellence and dedication in the performance of medical work. He said:

> Most doctors have no conception of hospital accounting . . . I have heard doctors say "I don't know a thing about my accounts; I let my secretary take care of it" . . . [This] is unbusinesslike . . . If a doctor is going to be in private practice, he must concern himself with practical matters . . . I think it not improper to have sound business methods.

Although this physician favored and did his own billing of patients, he did not claim that he was merely trying to be efficient. He regarded it also as fostering the public identification of the pathologist's services as being professional services; in the words of this pathologist, it demonstrated to patients that "there is a professional service involved." The entrepreneur felt that a concern with business efficiency, far from being detrimental to the reputation of medicine, would, in fact, lead to greater public confidence in the individual practitioner and medical practice in general. He believed that "[an] intelligent basis for facing financial aspects [of medical practice] leads to respect . . . for medical practice."

In summary, the entrepreneur's rationale for attending to business matters included its conduciveness to efficiency, its compatibility with excellence of task performance, and its furtherance of professional recognition and respect by the public. This involved an amalgamation of the roles of the technical expert and the administrative expert on the supposition that "attending to business matters" has professional and medical legitimacy. The amalgamation involves seeking professional justification for administrative, or business, activities. But it also involves seeking a mandate from the *general public*. It is the general public who pay the fee to the entrepreneur and, hence, it is the general public that must be convinced of the pathologist's professional stature when he is in independent practice. By contrast, the salaried pathologist receives his income from the hospital; he need not seek a mandate from the general public. Indeed, he welcomes his hospital tenure because it spares him from having to seek a public mandate.

The values expressed—by the salaried pathologist concerning his concentration on technical matters and by the entrepreneur concerning the incorporation of administrative matters—are reflected in the way their respective organizational arrangements include acceptance of external control and assertion of autonomy. The salaried pathologist's role is nurtured in the hospital context. The entrepreneur's role, which combines technical and administrative content in one role, needs active support from the general public as well as from professional colleagues.

It would be an oversimplification to say that the entrepreneur pathologist's need for a public mandate gives him little autonomy from the general public. He has much contact with the public. Hence he can be influenced by the public in many ways. But, in turn, he can influence the public's views about pathologists. In particular, he tries to promote the view that pathologists are as outgoing, as forthright, and as personable as other physicians. To accomplish this he engages in extensive participation in community affairs. In addition, in his direct contact with patients and their families, he lays much stress on having courteous and satisfying transactions.

Similarly, the salaried pathologist's apparent lack of autonomy from his hospital needs to be seen realistically. He has extensive interactions with his hospital's superintendent. Doubtless, the superintendent has much influence over the pathologist. But the pathologist also influences the hospital in a variety of ways. The corollary to this is that the entrepreneur has little interaction with hospital administrators and, in turn, has little influence upon them. A general hypothesis emerges: *A low degree of interaction has low potential for autonomy for the interacting parties. A high degree of interaction has a high potential for autonomy.* This means that the salaried pathologist has a low degree of autonomy in relation to the general public. To be sure, the public does not influence him in his day-to-day activities, and this makes it seem that he has a great deal of autonomy in relation to the public. But he, in turn, does not influence the public in any direct way.

His autonomy in relation to the public is minimal. In contrast, he seems to have little autonomy in relation to his administrator, with whom he has much interaction. Yet despite his subservience to the administrator's policies, he doubtless affects his hospital's policies in many ways. His actual autonomy in his hospital appears to be greater than the administrative arrangements make it seem. For instance, his technician-training program implies that he has control over a sizable portion of the hospital's funds; his active teaching pursuits within the hospital mean that he probably exerts considerable influence on the hospital's medical staff.

The fee-based pathologist occupies an intermediary position between the entrepreneur and salaried pathologist. He receives payment from the general public, that is, from individual patients; but the hospital, in handling the administrative aspects, acts as the intermediary between the pathologist and the public. The hospital provides a referral system and at the same time, permits the "private practice" benefits of individualized fees. The fee-based pathologist has autonomy patterns that combine the entrepreneur's active contact with the public and the salaried pathologist's influence within the hospital. He appears to have achieved the best of both worlds.

Remuneration: Salary, Fee, Percentage

The pathologist's way of receiving compensation—salary, fee, or percentage arrangement—highlights his way of coping with various professional and administrative conditions. Some pathologists regard the salaried pathologist as being in a "master-servant" relationship and speak of the impossibility of practicing unfettered medicine on a salary basis.[8] Many pathologists advocate fee or percentage arrangements because they believe that these arrangements provide the pathologist with an appropriate degree of control over the resources he needs to do his work and that such control constitutes the only ethical form of medical practice. Administrators tend to regard the fee-percentage efforts largely as harassment for the purpose of getting more income for pathologists.

A sociological interpretation of these efforts is that pathologists are using the remuneration issue as one of their tactics in an attempt to gain a social status that will be more nearly akin to that of the clinician than it is to the pathologist's traditional status.* This status would involve enhanced prestige for the pathologist. It would also give him a wider professional mandate by increasing his participation in clinical medicine.

Within the different remuneration arrangements examined by the case studies, different value was placed on fees and salaries. For example, the administrator of the salaried pathologist's hospital believed that aspirations for a fee or percentage arrangement are generally inspired by a desire for more income. Yet he attempted to cater to his pathologist's professional aspirations by giving him an increasing degree of control over laboratory income. The pathologist of this hospital expressed satisfaction with his salary arrangement, pointing out that he believed he could better serve the hospital on a salary. He stated:

> I'm content to work on a salary; there are so many things a pathologist should do for the good of the institution [hospital] and the medical profession for which there cannot be any remuneration. . . . [For instance] I'm administering the training of technicians, adviser to the resident staff . . . you can do a better job on these if you're not trying to get remuneration for each—on fee [basis] I'd be looking for making money all the time . . . maybe I'll change my mind sometime, but that's how I feel now.†

In short, he believed that a salary arrangement increased his autonomy in defining his technical obligations. He need not confine himself to those tasks for which a remuneration can be directly shown to exist.

This pathologist displayed awareness of the trend away from salaried arrangements and the presence of indirect pressure toward change in his form of employment. He noted, "Pressure comes from the College of American Pathologists and indirectly from your own colleagues that you know have different contracts." Fur-

---

* Another tactic is the effort to have more direct contact with patients.
† It must be emphasized that this physician did not claim that all those pathologists who are on a fee basis are primarily interested in "making money." He stated, merely, that he believed that if he were on a fee basis he would be "looking for making money all the time" at the expense of other duties.

ther, comparing himself with other pathologists, he stated, "I am interested to see how it all will come out . . . I know some of the people who are on fees make more money [than I do], but I doubt if they are any happier than I am."

The administrator of this hospital said that as far as he knew, the pathologist at his hospital was under no pressure to have a fee arrangement with the hospital: "If he is, he hasn't said anything about it." He reported that a "billing arrangement" had just been established for the hospital's radiologist, as a result of pressure upon the radiologist by his peers. Under this arrangement the hospital still does the billing of patients, but the bill now includes the radiologist's name. This suggests that the physician can utilize pressures from his professional peers outside the hospital as a lever in his dealings with the hospital administration. Evidently the situation at this hospital was not completely static in respect to the salary-fee controversy. But at the time of the study neither the pathologist nor the administrator was actively seeking a fee or percentage basis for the pathologist, although both men were attuned to the salary-fee arguments. The administrator was attempting to cater to the professional-status aspirations of the pathologist. The pathologist, in turn, was attempting to retain professional duties that he perceived to be threatened under fee arrangements.

The salary-fee situation between administrator and salaried pathologist seems to illustrate strategies and counterstrategies that enhance the autonomy of both. Neither side plays its trump cards. Yet each knows that the other has trump cards in reserve. On the basis of legal as well as sheer de facto power the administrator could have controlled the pathologist far more closely than he actually did. On the other hand, the pathologist could have pushed his claim for fees more strongly than he did; he was actually resisting pressures from his colleagues in pathology who urged him to get a fee arrangement. Although the administrator was not aware of the specific pressures, he was well aware of sentiments among many pathologists favoring fee arrangements. In this situation the administrator granted the pathologist a variety of professional powers, such as administering a technician-training program, that were somewhat peripheral to the purely technical execution of pathology work. The pathologist, in turn, acknowledged that the administrator had the final word on his salary and, indeed, on all financial matters in the hospital, at a time when many other physicians challenged such wide-ranging power by hospital administrators.

On a much larger scale, the strategy of gaining autonomy for both sides by not playing one's trump cards was employed during the epic confrontation between President Kennedy and Premier Khrushchev during the Cuban missile crisis. President Kennedy chose to blockade rather than invade Cuba on the assumption that blockade would not lead to immediate bloody contact between Americans and Russians and, in turn, would leave the Russians with some measure of autonomy. Hopefully, the American President reasoned, the Russians would use their autonomy to make a relatively graceful retreat. If bloody contact had occurred, each side might have been committed to an inexorable process of escalation toward nuclear war, where autonomy would have been absent for both sides and, therefore, the possibilities of de-escalation and a change of course would have been absent.

The entrepreneurial and fee-based pathologists strongly advocated the view that the pathologist's services are distinctly professional in nature and that the fee provides necessary and appropriate recognition. For example, concerning the billing of patients, the entrepreneur said, "Pathologists don't really want to bill patients; they want them to know that there is a professional service involved." He maintained, further, that in stressing the desire for recognition of his services as being professional, the pathologist does not want simply to imitate the clinician's work arrangement. This is, in any case, inherently impossible because of the differences in their respective tasks. Rather, the pathologist desires the prestige and concomitant privileges of a full-fledged physician: "The pathologist wants to be treated like a doctor." In pointing to the low status accorded to pathologists, he related the following story:

> There is the case of the old-time pathologist, a leader in the field. One day the administrator of the hospital called him and told him that he planned to have pictures taken of the heads of all departments at two o'clock that afternoon in a certain room, and would

he come. When the pathologist arrived at two, he found assembled there the chief janitor, chief linen service man, etc. He thought the administrator lacked tact; he would have preferred to have his picture taken with the chief of surgery.

The fee is seen as a means for overcoming this inadequacy of recognition. In the case of the entrepreneur, the recognition of the pathologist's individualized professional service is achieved by direct billing of patients. The fee-based pathologist's arrangement was made when he was first employed at the hospital. He was the first full-time pathologist at this hospital. Thus this hospital has apparently been spared the pains of making the pathologist's transition from a salaried "employee" to a "professional" paid from the income of the laboratory. It is likely that from these transitions, when the accustomed organizational patterns are changed, vested interests are most severely challenged and a residue of bitterness and anger is left behind.

The advocacy of the fee system raises the question of the justification of a fee, and, indeed, of the whole manner of remuneration for certain of the pathologist's professional functions. This applies especially to the supervision of laboratories and the performance of autopsies. Pathologists' views as to the *professional* nature of laboratory supervision vary with their own organizational relationships. Similarly, their estimates of the need for the routine performance of autopsies is related to their organizational commitments.

The *professional* character of laboratory supervision is questioned by the salaried pathologist but strongly affirmed by the fee-based and entrepreneurial pathologists. This alignment needs to be considered in conjunction with their respective forms of remuneration. The salaried pathologist's supervision of the laboratory is included in his general salary; the others receive a proportion of the income from the various tests that are performed in the laboratory. The fee-based and entrepreneurial pathologists contend that even though they do not personally observe the performance of each test, they do, nonetheless, exercise close professional influence and control. Thus, the entrepreneur pointed out that, with one statement, he can affect the entire course of his laboratory's procedures. The salaried pathologist mildly questioned this point of view. In contrast, a university pathologist stated bluntly, "I'd feel like a pimp, accepting a fee for every urinalysis!"

It is evident that the difference in perspective regarding the professional character of supervisory tasks parallels remunerative arrangements. The relationship between organizational arrangements and ideology—between the economic aspect of receiving payment for services defined as professional and the definition of laboratory supervision as being "professional"—is a question in the realm of the sociology of knowledge. The Marxian tradition of the sociology of knowledge, which has tended to dominate that field of sociology,[9] would maintain that the economic factor is likely to be the dominant feature. The definition of laboratory supervision as being professional would, thus, be *derived* from the pathologist's economic self-interest. Although this explanation has plausibility, it is necessary to point out that a counterargument could be given as follows: These physicians are eager to gain acknowledgment of their professional stature; for this reason they advocate that fees be paid for *all* their services, even those that might not have a very clear professional nature. The debate as to the origin of the ideology cannot be solved here. It can be indicated only that there is coherence and a degree of integration between the ideological and social organizational aspects and that these probably reinforce one another.[10]

A somewhat similar situation exists concerning the performance of autopsies. There is little question that performing autopsies is a distinctly professional task. But it is a task for which a fee cannot be charged: If a fee were charged, families would doubtless be even more reluctant to give permission for doing autopsies than they are at present. On the basis of their hospital arrangements, the fee-based and entrepreneurial pathologists are, therefore, not directly paid for this service.* The entrepreneur regards his charges for other work as covering autopsies. "In, say, hemoglobin, I may overcharge . . . there is no other way for the hospital to accumulate funds to pay me [for doing autopsies]." He

---

* However, they and the salaried pathologists get a fee for performing autopsies outside their hospital. This involves work at small hospitals or veterans hospitals where there is no full-time pathologist, or medicolegal autopsies for court cases.

believes that he does, in fact, receive payment for doing autopsies. The fee-based pathologist expressed the view that he is not being paid for performing autopsies; to him autopsies represent one way in which he repays the hospital for the privilege of using its facilities.

The pathologists held different views about the need for routinely performing autopsies. The entrepreneur and the salaried pathologist advocated the desirability of doing an autopsy on each deceased person in order to complete the medical procedures and to advance scientific knowledge. The fee-based pathologist, on the other hand, questioned the scientific usefulness of "doing autopsy after autopsy." He favored doing only those "which will benefit the doctor and the hospital."

Here again, a relation between ideology and organizational commitment is apparent: Pathologists who believe they receive payment for doing autopsies (the entrepreneur and the salaried pathologist) *can afford*, in the view of the economic-minded interpreter, to advocate doing autopsies on all deceased persons. But as in the laboratory situation, such a postulation may explain away too easily the ideological components of the situation. Also, there are technical medical differences of opinion about the usefulness of routinely performing autopsies on each deceased patient, although these are outside the social scientist's field of competence. The priority of the economic factors has not been proven, but there does exist congruence between organizational ideology and social arrangements.

Thus it seems that the precise terms of remuneration are by no means firmly established, but the underlying criteria are that the system of rewards recognize the dignity of the profession and be on a par with that of other medical practitioners. Pathologists are attempting, in the realm of remuneration as in other areas of administrative-professional relationships, to broaden their sphere of professional autonomy and recognition. As the entrepreneur stated, "The pathologist ought to make the same amount as a person with similar training . . . he is one of the better trained persons in the medical community." The percentage arrangement that the American College of Pathologists proposed is excellent, in the entrepreneur's view. But he regarded the size of the proposed income—40 percent of the laboratory's gross income—as "astronomical" unless shared by two or more pathologists.

In this connection, a hospital administrator expressed concern that a percentage arrangement for pathologists can lead to an "absolutely phenomenal" income. It is noteworthy that he voiced opposition not in terms of the loss of income to the hospital but in terms of the imbalance it would create within the medical profession.

Summary

It is important to remember that the salaried and fee-based pathologists represent practice in hospitals. They rely on the hospital's administration for providing administrative services. The laboratory equipment is owned by the hospital and the hospital employs the laboratory technicians. Hence, these pathologists are dependent upon the hospital in various ways. But in both the fee-based and salaried types, the administrative controls are accepted contingent upon what the pathologists consider proper recognition for their professional status.

For the salaried pathologist, professional recognition takes the form of the administrator's personal interest in providing him with adequate technical equipment, trained assistants, and a salary that the pathologist regards as adequate. This personal dependence, although satisfactory to the pathologist, is structurally tenuous: A new administrator might reverse the present administrator's policies. Of the three types of practice, the salaried pathologist emphasizes most the autonomy to concentrate on the "technical expert" role while trying to avoid as much as possible the "administrative expert" role. He is able to implement this in his work arrangements.

In contrast to the salaried pathologist's dependence upon the personal good will of the administrator, the fee-based pathologist enjoys formalized arrangements that assure recognition of his professional status. Examples of this recognition are the specific fee for each of his tissue examinations and the "professional factor" included in the fee for clinical tests to pay for his supervision of the laboratory. Also, the pathologist's services are specifically mentioned on patients' bills. These arrangements are incorporated into the pathologist's hospital contract and are, therefore, less subject to changes by an administrator than the salaried pathologist's arrangements. They are much more formalized guarantees to the pathologist's autonomy than the arrangements of the salaried pathologist.

The entrepreneurial form of practice constitutes the most independent form of administrative control by the pathologist himself. The pathologist owns the equipment he uses, employs his own assistants, and sets his own rates. He fuses the roles of "technical expert" and "administrative expert." He believes that physicians should concern themselves with "sound business" practices —this will create public confidence in their professional work. Concern with business matters need not interfere with doing excellent work.

The entrepreneur shares with the fee-based pathologist the conception of the fee as the most respectable form of professional remuneration. Although fees spur public recognition of the pathologist's contribution, thereby providing a public mandate, they involve corresponding risk factors in the collection of bills and income fluctuations based on public favor. The entrepreneur is more strongly affected by these factors than the fee-based pathologist (and, of course, much more than the salaried pathologist) because he does not have a monopoly of the work from a large hospital. The entrepreneur is thus most directly affected by the general public. His autonomy in administrative matters is counterbalanced by high dependence upon the general public and, as will be shown in the next section, by dependence on other physicians.

For the salaried pathologist the administrative functions are largely performed by the hospital. The hospital administrator personally guarantees professional prerogatives for the pathologist. For the fee-based pathologist the administrative functions are also largely performed by the hospital, but the pathologist's professional prerogatives are structurally embedded in the hospital's formal organization. The entrepreneur performs the administrative functions himself. His professional standing depends upon having the public and his medical colleagues accept his own enactment of administrative functions. In administrative matters he has clear autonomy, at least formally. The fee-based and salaried pathologists are, formally, subservient to their respective hospitals. But they have carved out for themselves distinctive ways of having autonomy within their hospital arrangements.

NOTES ...

1. Max Weber, "The Types of Authority and Imperative Co-ordination," *The Theory of Social and Economic Organization*, A. M. Henderson and Talcott Parsons, tr. (New York: Free Press, 1947), p. 324. Weber notes that "imperative control" (*Herrschaft*) involves "a certain minimum of voluntary submission."

2. Weber, "The Types of Authority and Imperative Co-ordination."

3. Fred E. Katz, "Pathologists, a Sociological Study of the Professional Relationships of a Medical Specialty" (Master's thesis, University of North Carolina, 1956), pp. 72–80.

4. *Ibid.*, Chap. II.

5. *Ibid.*, p. 41.

6. *Ibid.*, p. 43.

7. *Ibid.*, pp. 72–80. See also Israel Gerver and Joseph Bensman, "Toward a Sociology of Expertness," *Social Forces* (March 1954), pp. 226–235. These authors suggest that "expertise increasingly develops prestige and legitimacy, but the power and prestige of the individual working expert decrease" while that of the administrative expert increases.

8. It was not ascertained what proportion of the membership hold this view. Nor was it found what influence these individuals wield within the profession. Katz, "Pathologists, a Sociological Study," p. 81.

9. Robert K. Merton remarked that "Marxism is the storm-center of *Wissenssoziologie*." See Merton, *Social Theory and Social Structure* (New York: Free Press, 1957), p. 462.

10. The functional consequences and the genesis of ideologies have been the perennial concern of the sociology of knowledge. No decisive proofs have been developed. *Ibid.*, Part III.

6

Autonomy in Adapting
to Professional Colleagues

The growth of specialties in modern medicine has given rise to changing and at times vaguely defined relationships among members of the various specialties. A basic issue is the need to coordinate the work of practitioners who are increasingly specializing on limited portions of the total expanse of the existing knowledge. The problem is to clarify the professional domain of each specialty: What sort of independence must each specialty have? What sort of interdependence is there among specialties? In the care of patients there is obviously a great deal of functional interdependence of the specialties. But there are also centripetal forces at work that tend to emphasize continuing separation of specialties. These grow out of differences in responsibilities as well as differences in perspective to work tasks and differences of tradition. Instead of speculating about ideal solutions to the dilemmas, it will be useful to look at the actual strategies the pathologists use.

This will be done by examining the posture of the pathologists toward clinical medicine: In which ways do they assert autonomy? In which ways do they fuse their actions with those of clinicians? In which ways do they foster the autonomy of clinicians? Some answers will be provided by looking at the pathologist's accessibility to clinicians, his playing the part of "doctor's doctor," and his being a policeman toward clinicians.

Role Adaptation: Accessible Colleagues—Segregated Scientist

The old-time pathologist is stereotyped as a semirecluse who shuns contact with the hospital staff and is happy only when busying himself in the morgue or working with chemicals and tissue slides. He is believed to lack interest in clinical medicine.[1] A more positive view must give credit to pathologists having a tradition of interest in scientific matters that are removed from the immediate doctor-patient interaction but, nonetheless, have medical importance. The stereotype points up the fact that traditionally pathologists and clinicians had different medical interests and that pathologists tended to lack attunement to the conditions under which clinicians work. (Presumably clinicians have similarly lacked sympathetic attunement to the interests of the scientifically disposed pathologist.) Is the pathologist's lack of involvement in clinical pressures essential to his functioning as a scientist? Is a degree of detachment from clinical colleagues essential if the pathologist is to function as "policeman"? In short, what sort of autonomy does the pathologist need as he interacts with clinicians while trying to preserve his traditional functions?

The historical survey showed that pathologists' status efforts include emphasis on increased participation in, or at least attunement to, the clinical features of medicine as a means of getting greater professional recognition. In the case studies, all three types of pathologist have "accessible" relationships with clinicians. All three are in closer contact with clinical colleagues and their problems than the old stereotype suggests. All three receive numerous and varied requests from clinicians. As a result they may see patients at the bedside or in the operating room and suggest laboratory procedures and tissue examinations to the clinician.

The representatives of the three types are alike in having relatively amiable relationships with clinicians in the course of these transactions.

During the study, clinicians initiated virtually all professional interactions with the fee-based and salaried pathologists. The entrepreneur, on the other hand, engaged in active *seeking out* of clinicians and asked them about their problems with patients. In his own words, he daily "makes the rounds of doctors." This was evidently an essential aspect in a process of cultivating a clientele of physicians. It involved a deliberate effort to make himself congenial to clinicians.

The entrepreneur's active cultivation of contact with clinicians approached the polar opposite of the stereotyped "segregated scientist." It is noteworthy that of the three types of pathologist included in this study, the entrepreneur exhibited least participation in scientific research. He expressed no desire to do research, he had not recently completed any research work, and preferred scientific conferences of "people in practice" as against university conferences. He also had the lowest participation in "policing" activities. Conversely, the salaried and fee-based pathologists, whose colleagueship with clinicians rests on more passive ground, expressed strong desire to do research work. Their participation in policing functions is more active than that of the entrepreneur. Indeed, in the case of the fee-based pathologist there is a degree of zeal in this regard. This will be developed more fully in a later section.

Each of the two patterns—(1) active colleagueship with clinical practitioners combined with little participation in research and in policing of clinicians as well as (2) relative separation from clinicians combined with active participation in research and policing—can be thought of as a system. In the active-colleagueship pattern it is doubtless difficult to maintain sufficient social distance from clinicians to be effective in a policeman role. Also, in the attunement to clinical practice it is difficult to carry on much pure research; the pathologist lacks the time and, possibly, the inclination to pursue research that has no immediate clinical relevance. His rewards come from his clinical participation. In short, the parts are highly interdependent and mutually reinforcing.

They form a relatively distinct, autonomous system. Similarly, the separated-scientist pattern includes parts that are conducive to a self-sustaining system. The pathologist's research carries rewards in the form of recognition from pathologists in other hospitals. These interactions can provide the pathologist with sufficient social and psychological support so that he can remain relatively aloof from his clinical colleagues in his own hospital. This aloofness, in turn, can produce the social distance from clinicians that is necessary to be an effective policeman. And, being an active policeman may in turn produce further social distance from clinical colleagues. Here, then, is another system that contains mutually reinforcing parts that make it self-sustaining and, therefore, relatively autonomous from external influence to that system.

Role Adaptation: Doctor's Doctor

Sociologists emphasize that our cultural rules discourage the physician from having emotional involvement with his patients. In the words of Talcott Parsons, the physician is expected to be "affectively neutral" in his actions with patients.[2] But physicians encounter situations in which they may have inadequate knowledge or have no control over the course of events.[3] In these situations cool detachment is likely to be difficult. The problem is compounded by the fact that the clinician is usually not free to express the true scope of his own uncertainties to the patient. This is so because, in the culture of Western medical systems, the physician is expected to be a man of certainty—a combination of scientist and magician. Both physician and patient share this expectation. Were the physician to express the real scope of his uncertainties to the patient, he could easily set in motion disastrous self-fulfilling prophecies in the patient's course of illness. After all, the patient is expected to trust his physician rather than his own intuitions. When the physician's confidence fails, all is lost. From the side of the clinician, there exists a need to find a context, away from patients, where he has autonomy to express his own uncertainties and emotional involvement and where he can develop guidelines for a course of action.

The present studies suggest that the clinician seeks help from the pathologist during periods of uncertainty and disturbed emotion about patients. These efforts may be similar to the support the clinician seeks from any medical colleague. Yet there are also aspects in this transaction that relate especially to the pathologist's role and functions. It must be borne in mind that the pathologist sometimes evaluates the efforts of clinicians, especially those of surgeons. The steps that the clinician takes under conditions of uncertainty may later come under the judging eye of the pathologist. Thus, as a matter of precautionary strategy, the clinician is at times tempted to consult the pathologist during periods of uncertainty. In this regard a pathologist stated that on occasion he had received a telephone call from a clinician who explained that he was in a predicament and asked, "What will the tissue committee say if I adopt such and such a procedure?" Pathologists are reluctant to swallow this bait because once they do so, they are a party to the clinician's decisions. They would, then, lose all autonomy in their policing role. To be sure, pathologists are prepared to be consulted on clinical diagnoses. But when they have not seen the patient, or his laboratory specimen, they are most reluctant to let the clinician off the hook.

The pathologist is also used in the clinician's emotional involvements that cannot be expressed before the patient.* Being a physician who is not directly part of the clinical situation, the pathologist is, in a sense, the candidate *par excellence* before whom the clinical façade of supreme confidence may be dropped. Or stated in the words of a pathologist, "the clinician can admit to uncertainties and inadequacies to the pathologist in a manner he cannot do while he is with patients—before the patient they have to seem to know it all." Furthermore, there is indication that before the pathologist the clinician can enact some behavior, such as the expression of anger against a patient, which is inadmissible in the clinical situation.

An example of such emotional involvement, together with the way it differs from clinical behavior, is evident from an incident that occurred in the office of the salaried pathologist. In addition to the pathologist and the sociologist a physician doing residency work in pathology was also present: A surgeon came to the office

* It is not clear to what extent other doctors are also used for this purpose.

to inquire about the analysis of tissue that he had removed from a female patient on the previous day. He was told that the tissue analysis indicated advanced cancer, and after he looked at the slide through the microscope, the following conversation between the surgeon and the resident ensued:

SURGEON: She's had symptoms for five years, but hasn't seen a doctor. I delivered this woman ten years ago, and she hasn't seen a doctor since.

RESIDENT: Did you ask her why she waited so long?

SURGEON: [*mimicking patient*] "I was scared, doctor" . . . makes you mad . . .

RESIDENT: What are you going to do?

SURGEON: Tell her she has advanced cancer. Tell her husband her chances of recovery are about nil; we'll try deep X-ray and radium treatment if she can stand it, and if they have any plans for the two of them, they should carry them out now. [*Then, after asking the patholo-gist, "You don't mind if I use your phone, old boy?" the surgeon called the husband of the patient.*]

SURGEON: [*to patient's husband*] . . . we've got the microscopic report; it's as I told you the other day: your wife has very very extensive cancer, with it at this stage our only treatment is X-ray therapy; it'll eliminate her functions, no more chances of pregnancy—you know she's always afraid of pregnancy; well, there won't be any more danger of that . . . no one in the world will know how much good this will do . . . I told her the other day she had malignancy, very far advanced . . . vicious looking . . . only form of treatment is deep X-ray treatment, hoping we can . . . yes sir, it has already spread, all the way into the womb; I just don't know whether we can do anything; we'll see how she can tolerate X-rays, then we'll send her home if she can tolerate it; all right Mr.——.

These guarded statements vary both in factual emphasis as well as in emotional content from those made to the pathologist. While talking with the pathologist the surgeon expressed anger at the patient for not having sought treatment earlier and a sense of resignation and failure about her fate: "her chances of recovery are about nil." In conversation with the husband, however, he dwelled on *treatment* methods and on the likely loss of reproductive functions rather than on loss of life itself.

While the pathologist thus serves as "doctor's doctor" to the clinician, he may, at the same time, act as "teacher" and "policeman." This can be illustrated from an interaction that took place between the entrepreneur pathologist and a surgeon:

> Upon the pathologist's arrival at the small hospital one morning there was a surgeon waiting for him in the laboratory. The surgeon had taken out the stomach of a seventy-year-old man during the night. The patient had been suffering from ulcers. The operation was completed around 1:00 A.M. Shortly after the operation, the patient had begun to bleed through a tube from the mouth and the bleeding failed to stop. Continuous blood transfusions were administered. The patient went into a state of shock. The surgeon related that he had been with the patient almost the whole night. He wanted the pathologist to help him find out whether the patient had a blood clotting defect—"his brother was here last year and he bled for three days"—or whether to operate in order to check for any blood vessels which might not have been sealed off or had burst since the operation. An operation was risky in view of the patient's advanced age and weakened condition. Samples of the patient's blood had been brought to the laboratory, and the surgeon and the technician had examined them. The surgeon said he "can't find anything the matter" with the patient, but the blood simply would not clot.

> While relating the events and throughout the pathologist's subsequent action the surgeon was in a highly agitated state. He alternately paced the floor and abruptly sat down, propping his legs on a nearby table.

> In contrast to the surgeon's excited movements the pathologist was a picture of utter composure. In quiet fashion he began making blood clotting tests. The technician had said that the blood did not have enough platelets. [Platelets are required for blood coagulation.] After studying the blood under a microscope the pathologist said, "There are plenty of platelets." He then asked the surgeon and the technician to look at the slide under the microscope. He then asked the technician from which arm the sample of blood had been taken. It turned out that she had obtained it from the

same arm on which the transfusion was being given. [The blood sample was evidently tapping the transfusion blood which presumably had been treated with anticoagulants.] The pathologist then ascertained from the surgeon that the patient's blood had clotted around the wound and had been clotting during the operation.

While some of the tests were in progress the pathologist examined the stomach which had been removed. Upon opening the stomach, it became apparent that the ulcer was exceedingly small. The pathologist said to the surgeon, in a good-natured tone, "I hope when my ulcer is that small you won't take out the whole stomach." The pathologist and the surgeon then went to the patient's room [the sociologist did not accompany them]. Upon their return the surgeon thanked the pathologist, and after saying, "I am tired . . . I am a little tired of this patient . . . I was ascared [sic] this morning" he left to perform another operation on the patient.

On the following day the pathologist visited the patient again. This time the crisis was over; the patient was no longer bleeding, and no longer in a state of shock.

Here the pathologist acted as "doctor's doctor." This may be distinguished from purely technical "consultation" in that the pathologist concerned himself with more than the limited problem of whether the blood of the patient clotted properly. He visited the patient, he provided the surgeon with a setting in which he could "let off steam," he censured the surgeon for removing an entire stomach on the basis of a very small ulcer, and he taught the surgeon and the laboratory technician something about blood coagulation.

One can view this transaction as a situation in which services were exchanged between the pathologist and the surgeon. The pathologist came to the scene when the surgeon was badly in need of knowledge that only the pathologist could provide. The surgeon's freedom to maneuver, his autonomy, was severely curtailed. The pathologist was in a position to charge a high price. The fee he would charge the patient was but one item in the transaction; he could also afford to charge the surgeon a price. The latter price included the exercise of the role of teacher and policeman, both of which are intrusions upon the surgeon's sphere of autonomous judgment. Concerning the teacher role, it will be recalled that the pathologist asked the surgeon to look at a sample of the blood under the microscope to see that it did, in fact, contain sufficient blood-clotting elements (platelets). The surgeon had already studied microscope slides of the patient's blood before the pathologist had arrived. Now he was being told to look again in order to learn that his previous assessment was in error. This, surely, is an intrusion into the surgeon's professional autonomy. Similarly, the remark "I hope when my ulcer is that small you won't take out the whole stomach" is a piece of unmistakable censure that cuts into the surgeon's sphere of autonomous judgment.

The transaction suggests that one man's loss of autonomy can be another man's gain. The surgeon was, temporarily at least, in a position of low autonomy and the pathologist was able to benefit by increasing his own autonomy. The pathologist used this autonomy to go beyond the purely technical tasks and enact some of the traditional pathologist functions, that of policeman and teacher of scientific medicine. One cannot assume that this one incident will necessarily make a permanent change in the relationship between this pathologist and surgeon. The point of the illustration is to show that in a particular transaction the presence or absence of autonomy influences the ingredients that are available for exchange.

Finally, how do the three pathologists differ in regard to the "doctor's doctor" functions? All three rejected the conception that the pathologist is infallible. They believe clinicians hold exaggerated conceptions about the pathologist's capacity for taking care of the clinician's uncertainties. On the other hand, they provide clinicians with a context for the expression of sentiments that cannot be expressed in the clinical situation.

The enactment of the "doctor's doctor" functions is facilitated for the salaried and fee-based pathologists by virtue of their being permanently located in their respective hospitals. The clinicians in these hospitals come to the laboratory and discuss their problems. In the case of the salaried pathologist this resulted in frequent visits by clinicians; sometimes the issues concerned crucial problems of particular patients, sometimes the discussions roamed over general clinical concerns. In the situation of the fee-based pathologist the visits by clinicians were less frequent and usually focused on specific problems. It is possible that the more formal relationships of the fee-based pathologist with clinicians was due to this pathologist's more active participation and far "tougher" stand in policing functions than that of the salaried pathologist.

The entrepreneurial pathologist compensated for his lack of permanent location in one hospital by his practice of seeking out clinicians and asking them about their problems. They also contacted him by phone when he was not at the hospital at the time crises occurred. Of the three pathologists studied, he made the most explicit statement that his function was to *serve clinicians* and that by serving clinicians he is serving patients. For him the "doctor's doctor" role was the most important role. For this purpose he made an effort to be maximally accessible to clinicians, involving a most energetic use of coffee breaks. The role also involved a de-emphasis of judgmental or policing functions that might alienate clinicians from the pathologist. The salaried and fee-based pathologists also engaged in the "doctor's doctor" role but gave it less prominence in view of their competing commitments to other functions.

Policing Functions of Pathologists

As we have seen, the pathologist is occasionally in a position to uncover errors made by his clinical colleagues. This may occur as he studies surgically removed tissue and as he performs autopsies on deceased patients. Traditionally, the pathologist has been viewed as a kind of policeman within the medical profession, whose findings constitute the ultimate review of clinical work. Our survey indicated, however, that there was no agreement within the medical profession, and among pathologists themselves, as to how the pathologist should handle his policing relationship toward clinicians. Should he be a severe critic? Should he be a teacher, who demonstrates mistakes as part of the process of learning? Should he be set apart as the infallible and superior judge, or should he, himself, be regarded as fallible and a student rather than a teacher? [4] The survey also showed that in communicating his findings to clinicians and in trying to assure future corrective measures, the pathologist was at times faced with antagonism and embarrassment. This was most likely to occur when a high-ranking surgeon was the offending party. Finally, it was noted that the establishment of tissue committees made up of representative groups of the medical staff has lessened the "judgmental" tasks of pathologists. These committees meet periodically to make evaluations of discrepancies between the original diagnosis made by the clinician and the final diagnosis made by the pathologist.

The issue of tissue evaluation illustrates that among medical specialties the professional domains overlap. Antagonisms are the manifestations of wounded claims to areas of autonomy. More specifically, what a pathologist may regard as his legitimate and necessary evaluative duties may be regarded by surgeons as infringement upon their professional independence. Among multiple specialties within a profession such intrusions and conflicting legitimacies are to be expected.

But the relation of the pathologist to surgeons is not a mere case of overlapping of competence between different specialties. It is a situation where certain basic professional activities of one specialty are thought to be regulating, or "policing," another specialty. That is, the professional tasks of one specialty become a threat to another specialty.

All the pathologists in the case studies avowed that it was not the pathologist's function to act as judge of his medical colleagues, that many of the "policeman" descriptions in the literature were exaggerations of what the majority of pathologists actually do, and that the pathologist was by no means infallible. Despite this agreement among the pathologists, it will be instructive to describe and analyze how they view and participate in policing activities. The focus will be on participation in the work of tissue committees.

At the salaried pathologist's hospital there is a tissue committee that was established and operated by the surgeons. The pathologist reported that he had not desired to be a member of this committee and joined it only recently. He joined at the suggestion of a member of a visiting team from the American College of Surgeons, which was conducting an investigation for

purposes of ascertaining the hospital's suitability for a residency
program in surgery. It was suggested that the pathologist become
an ex-officio member of the committee, that is, a member without
the privilege of voting. Concerning his lack of a vote, the pathologist said, "I think that [is] a very good arrangement. It keeps
the pathologist off the spot. Some surgeons might think the
pathologist was out to get them. If he has no vote this is difficult
to demonstrate." He felt that the matter of voting is of little
importance as long as the pathologist "can really influence the
members of the committee." Thus he tried to avoid the charge of
interfering in the domain of surgeons, while actually trying to
exert policing influence. He stated that the pathologist's functions
on the tissue committee are:

1. To interpret the tissue reports [which he has submitted], if this
   is necessary. And, often, to point out the limitations of the
   pathologist's work—how much it is a matter of opinion, what
   would be stated differently by different pathologists.
2. We ought to help defend this guy as well as incriminate him.
3. For us to learn. We get very limited clinical information . . .
   the man in the best position to make the diagnosis, as a rule, is
   not the pathologist but the clinician. He has most information
   about the patient.

It was his opinion that in most instances the discrepancies between the diagnosis of the pathologist and the clinician could be
readily justified without claiming that negligence or incompetence
are involved. Finally, he said that he did not know what actions
the committee had taken in cases of unjustified discrepancies.

It is evident that the salaried pathologist desires only a limited
part in the proceedings of the tissue committee and virtually no
part in any punitive actions that the committee might take against
a physician. He is eager not to be regarded as wishing to infringe
upon the domain of surgeons or having the pathologist regarded
as being a superior diagnostician. Nevertheless, he wants the
pathologist to have a hearing.

In contrast to the salaried pathologist, the fee-based pathologist takes an active part in the actions of the tissue committee
of his hospital. Indeed, he founded the committee, after engaging

the support of the trustees of the hospital. He reported that he decided to follow the procedural guide of the American College of Surgeons, including sending very forthright letters to the physicians involved in questionable work. The pathologist said that he did not have himself named as chairman of the committee so that the physicians might regard the committee as an agency of the medical staff rather than as the "pathologist's committee." Nonetheless, it is the pathologist who dictates the letters that are sent out by the committee. The committee meets in the pathologist's office. And the pathologist is the only permanent member of the committee.

The pathologist stated that it was the function of the committee to review all normal tissue that was surgically removed; all tissue that, upon microscopic examination, differed from the clinical diagnosis; all cases where operations were performed and no tissue was removed; and "particular scrutiny [was given to] gynecologic surgery and appendectomies." At the time of the case studies, the committee had not taken any disciplinary measures against physicians other than sending letters to them. The pathologist stated that further disciplinary measures might be taken at a future date "when the pattern is set as to who gets letters."

The forthright nature of the letters can be illustrated from excerpts of letters which were actually sent:

. . . this record was reviewed because a normal appendix had been removed in a young female. The abdomen is completely devoid of any inflammation that would suggest appendicitis as a possible diagnosis. We note a primary and final diagnosis of internal appendicitis. On the basis of the data information we consider this surgery entirely and completely unjustified.

Sincerely,
THE TISSUE COMMITTEE

. . . we therefore feel that this surgery was not justified . . .

. . . we are distressed beyond measure that in view of a normal appendix, the final record reads subacute appendicitis . . .

It is apparent, then, that the fee-based pathologist is very actively enacting a policeman role within the medical community of his hospital, although he does not wish to have it labeled as such.

It is perhaps not surprising to find that this makes him somewhat less than popular among surgeons. The pathologist noted that since morphology is "the last court of appeal," the pathologist is "automatically unpopular." And "when in staff meetings they raise hell about the committee they always look at me [although other members of the committee are present]; they take it for granted that the pathologist is trying to keep surgeons from doing surgery." What the pathologist here regards as his legitimate professional domain is evidently regarded as an infringement on their domain by surgeons. The professional prerogatives of one specialty interfere with the professional prerogatives of another specialty.

The pathologist regards the goal of the tissue committee to be the improvement of surgical work and considers it to have been a "terrific instrument for improving surgery." Table 4 is a record of the committee's accomplishments during its three years of operation. The pathologist does not regard the lower number of letters sent in the third year as a sign of lowering standards by the committee, but as an indication of improved surgery.

In pursuing its goal he feels that the tissue committee has steered a middle course between "covering up" for surgeons and being publicly offensive toward these physicians. He is anxious for the committee to be accepted as part of the medical staff's procedural devices and to drop its label as "the pathologist's committee." When, and if, this is accepted, the onus of being a "policeman" might conceivably be removed from the shoulders of the pathologist.

In summary, the fee-based pathologist has initiated a tissue committee that has the improvement of surgery as its main goal. This is in implementation of the pathologist's discovery of surgical errors in the course of his morphological work. In contrast to his salaried counterpart, the fee-based pathologist is acknowledging the pathologist's discovery of errors and the need for regulatory devices. He does not regard surgeons' claims of professional interference as justified and, thanks to the backing of the trustees, he does not fear their wrath. However, the label "policeman" is one that he does not relish. While rejecting the *label* of policeman he is, in fact, carrying out the *role* of policeman. The salaried

Table 4.

YEAR OF TISSUE COMMITTEE'S ACTION	MAJOR OPERATIONS PERFORMED IN THE HOSPITAL	CASES REVIEWED BY THE TISSUE COMMITTEE	LETTERS SENT TO SURGEONS BY THE TISSUE COMMITTEE
1st year	1126	91	2 doctors each received 15 letters
			2 doctors each received 5 letters
			1 doctor received 2 letters
			3 doctors each received 1 letter
2nd year	1223	74	1 doctor received 7 letters
			1 doctor received 5 letters
			2 doctors each received 4 letters
			2 doctors each received 1 letter
3rd year	1455	47	1 doctor received 8 letters
			1 doctor received 6 letters
			3 doctors each received 1 letter

pathologist, it will be recalled, avoids both label and role by defining his duties in terms of advisory services to the clinician— "[who is] in the best position to make the diagnosis."

Another way of avoiding both the role and label of policeman is presented when the presence of overriding conditions in a hospital spare the pathologist from having to act as policeman. This is evident in the entrepreneur's preference for working at small hospitals.* He reports that a small Catholic hospital is "a nice place for a pathologist to work" because the "attitude toward life" largely assures the absence of sterilizations and unnecessary hysterectomies. He notes, also, that a small hospital generally offers a good situation for the pathologist because physicians recognize that its existence is sufficiently precarious even without endangering its accreditation through possible charges of unnecessary surgery.

The entrepreneur's participation in policing functions in the hospital for which he is the pathologist is essentially advisory in character. He is the only permanent member on the tissue committee, whose members are annually chosen by the chief of service and whose chairman is usually a surgeon. During meetings of the committee the pathologist reads the case aloud, omitting the names of the patient and doctor, and the committee tries to reach a decision that is "as objective as possible." The committee itself takes no direct action against a physician but, instead, refers its findings to the hospital's executive committee. At the time of the study, the pathologist was not a member of the executive committee. Thus, while the pathologist participates in fact-finding and evaluation, he does not take direct part in punitive aspects of policing activities.

The avoidance of "policing" is probably particularly crucial in the case of the entrepreneur. The alienation accompanying policing activities would hardly be conducive toward establishing a voluntary clientele of physicians. And, as noted earlier, such a clientele is a central feature of the entrepreneur's practice. The fee-based pathologist, on the other hand, has less need to rely on

---

* His work at hospitals is carried on in addition to his practice in the laboratory that he owns.

the good will of a clientele, since his hospital provides him with a monopoly of the pathology work and a powerful professional status. The salaried pathologist is somewhere in between. He has a virtual monopoly of the hospital's pathology work, but his position is not as firmly established as that of the fee-based pathologist. His participation in policing functions reflects this condition, as well as his own view of the limitations of the pathologist's professional responsibilities. In sum, pathologists' autonomy in carrying out policing activities is limited not only by their ethic concerning their professional responsibility but by the total structural arrangements of their practice.

Summary

All three types of practice are geared to active cooperation with clinicians, but the techniques for carrying it out differ. The entrepreneur was most active in seeking accessibility to clinicians and participating in clinical medicine. He actively cultivated clinicians as a clientele by making daily "rounds of doctors" in the hospitals with which he was associated and by emphasizing his accessibility at all times. He explicitly stated his main task was to be "serving the doctors." He tried to minimize those functions that might interfere with this conception of his role. These include those functions, such as "policing" and teaching, that might place the pathologist in superordinate rather than coequal relationship to clinicians.

In short, the entrepreneur exercised great autonomy in initiating interactions with clinicians. But this autonomy includes sacrifice of the traditional scope of these interactions. In the pathologist's traditional policing activities, this pathologist enjoys little autonomy.

The fee-based and salaried pathologists did not actively seek out clinicians although, by having permanent quarters in their respective hospitals, they have a degree of accessibility to clinicians that the entrepreneur does not have. They both seek to render service to clinicians, but (unlike the entrepreneur) they also participate in such nonclinical functions as research and teaching.

The fee-based pathologist actively enacts policing functions and has had open battles with clinicians over his policing activities. He has been supported in these efforts by the hospital's trustees. His professional support derives less from a voluntary medical clientele than from the nonmedical hospital authorities.

In summary, he has considerable autonomy from control by clinicians. Yet he participates in a broad range of clinical activities —both direct clinical services and traditional policing and teaching services. This is accomplished by accepting subservience to a strong, nonmedical hospital administration.

The salaried pathologist, just as the entrepreneur, encourages a voluntary mandate from clinicians. But unlike the entrepreneur he seeks his professional mandate within one particular hospital. He encourages clinicians' informal visits. (By contrast, clinicians' visits to the office of the fee-based pathologist tend to be rare and, when they do occur, they usually involve a relatively specific formal consultation.) The salaried pathologist tries to avoid policing functions, although he wishes the pathologist "to be heard" at hearings of the tissue committee. His professional support is evidently derived from both the hospital as well as professional colleagues. He seeks to carry out a broad range of professional tasks—traditional policing, clinical assistance in the immediate treatment of patients, as well as long-range research. In an age of specialists this pathologist tries to remain a competent generalist. The scope of his professional role is probably even broader than that of the fee-based pathologist. To achieve the necessary autonomy for a broad technical scope, he accepts a degree of subservience both to his hospital's administration and to clinicians. He accepts the employee-of-the-hospital status at a time when other physicians seek the status-giving halo of professional fees. He wants to influence clinicians but does not assert himself over them in policing activities.

Finally, the adaptations of pathologists doubtless affect the autonomy of clinicians. A full-scale study of the autonomy of clinicians was not undertaken. But it seems that the entrepreneurial and salaried pathologists provided surgeons with a haven for giving vent to their uncertainties and expressing emotions that are taboo around patients.

NOTES ...

1. See, for example, J. D. Arnaud, "Pathology in Clinical Practice," *Caribbean Medical Journal*, 16 (1954), 1–2; and David Riesman, "Men and Events in the History of the Philadelphia Pathological Society," *Annals of Medical History*, N. S., 6 (1954), 359–375.
2. Talcott Parsons, *The Social System* (New York: Free Press, 1951), p. 435.
3. *Ibid.*, p. 450. Fred Davis has studied the "uncertainty factor" in terms of its impact on treatment processes; see "Uncertainty in Medical Prognosis: Clinical and Functional," *American Journal of Sociology*, LXVI, 1 (July 1960), 41–47.
4. The pathologist's role as "judge" or "policeman" received more emphasis in writings intended for consumption by the general public than in writings addressed to physicians. See Fred E. Katz, "Pathologists, a Sociological Study of the Professional Relationships of a Medical Specialty" (Master's thesis, University of North Carolina, 1956), pp. 62–63.

7

Autonomy within the University

Professionals do not merely dispense knowledge. They create knowledge. Nowhere is this more evident than in university centers, where research typically has a prominent place. The social conditions that are conducive to doing research work are not necessarily conducive to doing applied professional work. Conversely, the social climate that is suitable to the practice of a profession may be ill suited for supporting research. Universities are centers of research as well as teaching centers for practitioners who are expected to be skilled in the art of dispensing a body of knowledge. University hospitals manifest the dilemma with an added twist. They are centers of medical research, centers of teaching, and at the same time treatment centers for persons who are ill. Not only is there a question of how well suited the research-minded professor is for training persons who will be practitioners in a clinical situation. There is also a question of how well and how enthusiastically the research-minded professor performs clinical functions in his own university setting. Clinical and research interests are apt to intrude upon each other. Yet each must have some autonomy if it is to be pursued at all. The spheres in which autonomy is asserted will be taken as indicators of professional emphasis and of the ways in which the cross-pressures are reconciled.

As knowledge-producing centers, universities are in the forefront of the proliferation of specialties. In university hospitals far more medical specialization is encountered than in average general hospitals. The development of new specialists requires autonomy to pursue and strengthen a particular sphere of knowledge. But a specialty only becomes practically significant when it is accepted by the existing practitioners. In short, the specialist is highly interdependent with other professionals at the same time that he must have autonomy in his specialized sphere of technical competence.

University pathologists exhibit the academician's dilemma between research and practice—the specialist's need for independence from as well as interdependence with professional colleagues, and the status problems of pathologists already discussed. In general, these pathologists seek autonomy in the technical realm and accept outside control in the administrative realm. But there is considerable variability among university pathologists, especially in terms of the balance that is struck between research, clinical, and teaching functions. There is much awareness that new specialties, such as bacteriology, make inroads on old specialties, such as traditional morphological pathology. In this chapter we shall consider the adaptations of university pathologists to the various dilemmas that confront them.

The departments of pathology of three universities were included in our study. Unlike the one- or two-man operations of pathologists in the nonacademic arrangements described previously, each academic department contained five or more physicians. Each department included a salary arrangement for its pathologists. In one department the salary comprised the total income for the pathologists, covering teaching and clinical-service functions. Another department had a modification of the salary arrangement, with a salary for teaching, research, and intramural medical services and fees for extramural medical work. The members of the third department, which we shall refer to as the entrepreneurial department, received a salary to cover teaching, research, and supervision of clinical pathology laboratories; they received fees from intramural and extramural morphological work. The extramural work involves tissue work for physicians from surrounding counties and even from other states. It is a large entrepreneurial enterprise and is the chief source of income for members of this department.

The chairman of the salaried department expressed annoyance with his "employee-of-the-hospital" arrangement. He said that such an "employee" arrangement indicated a low degree of recognition for the pathologist's professional functions. He is eager to change the remuneration arrangements in order to produce greater recognition of the pathologist's professional contribution. To improve the pathologist's professional mandate, he advocated that pathologists receive a portion of the income from the hospital's private diagnostic clinic, stating: "Other doctors get income from this source, but pathologists don't." But this was rejected: "The university wants [pathologists] to stay on full-time [salary basis] . . . [this] is exploitation of professional service." What induces pathologists to remain in such a situation at a time when there is a shortage of pathologists and they could easily get work elsewhere? The redeeming feature seems to lie in the teaching and research opportunities. Strong interest in teaching and research was mentioned by each university pathologist, including the members of the above chairman's department. In contrast, that chairman was the only one who expressed dissatisfaction with the salary arrangement. Several pathologists outside the university centers expressed dissatisfaction with academicians' acceptance of salary arrangements. One of these stated that while university pathologists generally support fee advocacies, they "somehow" exempt themselves. Apparently university pathologists place research and teaching functions ahead of concern with the "salaried-employee" condition.

Relationships with Medical Colleagues

The three types of pathologists who are practicing outside universities emphasize that the pathologist should provide services that are of practical and immediate usefulness to the clinician. They believe that the pathologist must consider himself part of the clinical process, that he must be readily available to clinicians, and that his reports must be furnished rapidly and in a form that has practical applicability to the treatment of the individual patient. This, of course, constitutes a rapprochement to the operating pressures of the clinician on the part of these pathologists. It involves, at the same time, pathologists' willingness to renounce a degree of autonomy for carrying on nonclinical functions. Among the university pathologists, especially the salaried ones, there is far less rapprochement to the world of the clinician. Nonclinical functions receive a great deal of emphasis.

The academic pathologist's ways of making diagnoses show his divergence from his colleagues in clinical areas. The pathologist responsible for most autopsy reports at one university stated that a typical challenge by clinicians, following his report, was "You haven't told me why this man died!" In reply, he said, "I answer, 'all morphological processes I have shown are incompatible with life; I don't know what caused death or, for that matter, what caused life.'" Further, concerning clinicians' demands for definiteness he stated, "[this is] the frustration of man wanting help; [he] can't call on the Lord, so he calls on the pathologist."* The surgical pathologist from another university reported that he is opposed to dogmatism on diagnoses, although surgeons seem to expect it, and that "instead of 'diagnoses' we give them 'interpretations.'" On the basis of difficulties encountered over this he now sends two decisions for each consultation; one is geared to readily "fitting into a pigeonhole" and the other is based on "looking at it academically." The latter contains ramifications and possibilities that may be relevant but do not necessarily lend themselves to immediate clearcut conclusions.

---

* The nonacademic pathologists also considered clinicians' demands for certainty of diagnoses to be excessive. But nonacademic pathologists appear to cater to the needs of clinicians more than do the academic pathologists.

Another illustration of the disparity between the academic pathologist and the "immediacy" demands of the clinician may be seen in the views about performing autopsies at night. A university autopsy pathologist reported that "clinicians gripe if we are not immediately available" for doing autopsies during the night. He said that it is preferable to do autopsies during the day because a pathologist called out during the night might forget items and that the presence of other staff members during the day makes consultations more feasible. All this is geared to "our main goal . . . which is complete study." The "complete study," with its concern for describing all physical characteristics of the deceased, is a much broader goal than is usually held by clinicians. Clinicians are mainly interested in discovering the cause of death.

These illustrations point to the academic pathologist's adherence to the scientific and scholarly exactitude of the researcher and thinker while participating in the professional activity of the practitioner. The intellectual profundity of the scholar is not necessarily geared to solving the issues facing the clinical practitioner. The clinician must not only face the intellectual challenge of correct diagnosis and devising effective therapeutic measures, he must also produce confidence in the patient. The patient's confidence is influenced by the doctor's own confidence. In this situation the clinician cannot afford to have a disposition to being continually uncertain. He is often under obligation to take immediate steps, even when he realizes that he lacks adequate knowledge. No wonder that he wants *definiteness* from the pathologist. The disposition to skepticism can be disastrous for accomplishing his tasks. On the other hand, the disposition to skepticism is at the heart of the role of the scholar-scientist.[1] The autonomy to remain skeptical is a precondition to his effectiveness in that role.

The lack of a common orientation between pathologist and clinician is striking in view of the fact that both are academicians. In modern universities, especially American universities, the practitioner and the scholar-scientist coexist. The difference between them tends to be overlooked in the view that, being academicians, they can perform both tasks. The academician is not only expected to teach future practitioners; he may also act as consultant on very practical matters, within or outside his university. Furthermore, academicians in applied fields—dentistry, social work, engineering, education—make efforts to do fundamental scholarly research. Whether this fusion of the purely scholarly with the practical problem solving is a happy marriage is by no means clear. Historically one might link the development of this pattern to the American bent for practicality and democratic equalitarianism: scholars are expected to be men of this world. Sociologically, one must ask whether the fusion of the roles of scholar-scientist and practitioner is effective in preserving, if not maximizing, the necessary contributions of each. In actuality, many an academician does effective scholarly work while, at the same time, doing an effective job of training practitioners and giving useful advice on the practical application of his knowledge. Yet there are also many instances where academicians accept consultation assignments on practical problems with only the remotest likelihood that they will bring to bear reasonably relevant practical skills and knowledge. Their stock recommendation is that more research is indicated, more conferences are needed, and so on. Theirs seems to be the outlook of the scientist who, when thrown into a practical situation, cannot make decisions before all the variables are fully controlled. The other side of the same picture is that sometimes long-term scientific projects are begun under the pressure of immediate, practical considerations. Whether it is a politically motivated race to the moon or an attempt to elevate the status of an occupation by showing that one can obtain research grants, research projects are often undertaken—money is obtained, people's professional careers are enlisted—with only slight relevance to fundamental scientific issues. To be sure, important scientific findings may occasionally emerge from such projects. The history and folklore of science is full of examples of accidental discoveries. But the pursuit of accidental discoveries is surely a very inefficient way of advancing fundamental knowledge.

If it is correct to say that the scholar-scientist and the clinical practitioner must necessarily bring a different outlook to their respective tasks, then surely their roles must be separated. Each role must have a degree of autonomy from the other. This point needs to be emphasized because the other side of the argument, the interdependence of research and application, is amply reiterated in present-day Western countries and tends to be accepted uncritically. Finally, it must be understood that the sociological statement that two roles are different does not mean that the same person cannot learn to perform both roles. It does mean that different social conditions are necessary for the enactment of the different roles.

Policing Functions in the Academic Context

Policing functions of pathologists blend into the academic medical culture. In this culture various evaluation procedures are well established. They include teaching sessions, close supervision of residents and medical students by senior physicians, and case conferences attended by staff members of all levels. The evaluation procedures are justified in terms of their teaching function and the general advancement of knowledge. In the course of the case studies it was found that pathologists cast their policing activities into these academically respectable terms. This was combined with efforts at avoiding duties that might interfere with being accepted as a co-academician by clinical colleagues.

There were no tissue-evaluation committees in the sampled universities, but there were autopsy conferences at which the pathologist gave a report in conjunction with reports by members of the clinical staff. At each university some pathologists expressed the view that in academic hospitals the quality of medical practice is high and that there is, therefore, no need for tissue committees. As one pathologist put it, "there is no tissue committee here . . . the purpose of a tissue committee is to safeguard the patient against indiscriminate procedures . . . no such danger exists in an academic situation." But policing obligations cannot be avoided altogether because there is awareness of occasional discrepancies between the pathologist's findings and the clinician's diagnoses, both in autopsies and in examination of surgically removed tissue. Reactions to such situations include various forms of refraining from a judgmental point of view while, nonetheless, recognizing that errors were made. Included are the notions that even when the general caliber of medical work is excellent, error is possible, and that the complexity of medicine is so great that error is possible even without actual negligence. Thus, regarding autopsy conferences, a pathologist reported:

> I see [clinicians] in stressful moments for them . . . The tone of the conference is largely set by the pathologist; I don't have it in me to call them rascals . . . I can see how it can come about . . . only in a few cases [are there disagreements] . . . If I thought they were willfully doing this I'd be upset . . . some pathologists at some places build up a lot of spleen . . . [it is] vastly different in a school . . .

Another similarly dispassionate reaction is that of the pathologist who regards himself as a consultant rather than a policeman:

> I used to get wrought up [over disagreement with surgeons] . . . not now . . . I am not in a position to force my opinion on them . . . I am looking on my role as that of consultant . . .

A further reaction consists in the advocacy that pathologists should avoid a judgmental attitude altogether and that their conferences with clinical colleagues should serve primarily a mutual teaching-and-learning purpose, in which the pathologist must avoid making himself superior:

> The object [of sessions with clinicians] is never to point out that [such and] such was done wrong . . . it is a mutual learning exercise . . . [the] pathologist is in a position to criticize—hindsight is always available to him—this is not constructive; [he] shouldn't conceal errors . . . [but he should not] use it as a power mechanism to make himself seem more knowledgeable than the other fellow; the pathologist has retrospection always available to him, he has to avoid being real superior.

The adaptations cited point to an avoidance of an explicit policeman role by the pathologist in favor of an academic way of carrying out the regulative functions through teaching and learning, respect for diversity of views, as well as awareness of human frailties. The adaptations try to avoid setting the pathologist apart from his academic colleagues in a role that might occasionally require the pathologist to take a position of superiority toward his clinical colleagues. One way that lessens the "superordination" of the pathologist is that academic clinicians tend to have their own evaluation and teaching conferences. At one of the three universities a senior member of the surgery department was trained in pathology. In the words of the surgical pathologist at that university, the surgeons do not uncritically accept the pathologist's reports: "[The surgeon with pathology training] and I not infrequently interpret tissue differently." The pathologist accepts this as being fruitful; indeed, he facilitates it by accompanying his tissue reports with a tissue slide so that his diagnosis may easily be checked and reevaluated by his clinical colleague.

Avoidance of being a policeman over clinicians is expressed by another pathologist as follows:

> Our surgeons here are very competent; in some places surgeons are a stupid bunch . . . I'd hate to face that crowd in a tissue committee.

And

> We see much [clinical work] from small hospitals to know I wouldn't want to go [there] . . . keeps me in medical school [despite very tempting financial offers].

And

> [in private practice] you expend ninety percent of the time overcoming friction . . . I'd rather have close contact with disease than [contact with] rascals, ignoramuses . . .

In summary, the university pathologists strive for tranquil academic colleagueship with clinicians. Here criticism is accepted as long as it permits colleagues a degree of autonomy in making professional judgments, including the right to be wrong, occasionally. There is no one, autonomous policeman role. Instead, the pathologist's evaluations are combined with the evaluations by the other physicians that, collectively, make up the academic medical culture's ongoing emphasis on evaluation. Here the pathologist can actively participate in policing activities without being singled out for encroaching on the autonomy of clinicians. By renouncing the autonomy to be *the* policeman, the pathologist probably gains accessibility to his clinical colleagues and autonomy in his pursuit of the specialty's traditional interest in research.

The extensive evaluation processes in university-centered medical practice arrangements—the case conferences, the elaborate supervisory arrangements whereby senior staff checks junior staff, the numerous didactic consultation patterns—doubtless facilitate the teaching of medicine. But they are likely to perpetuate a degree of leisurely unreality as far as coping with immediate clinical issues. For the pathologist this sort of participation is apt to perpetuate his reputation for being hopelessly academic when trying to deal with practical clinical issues.

Research Emphasis—Clinical Emphasis

Implicit in preceding sections is the observation that academic pathologists have preserved interests that have very limited relevance to immediate clinical practice. While participating in clinical medicine they are, at the same time, trying to have some detachment from clinical pressures. Conversely, while doing research they are, at the same time, under pressure to concern themselves with immediate clinical matters.

The academician's desire for a degree of detachment from the tempo and pressures of clinical medicine is probably implicit in his preference for doing research work. But it is also made quite explicit by some academicians, as the following statements show. An academic pathologist who was formerly a general practitioner stated that in private practice he was "too rushed . . . no time to think." His main professional interests are "teaching, thinking, and research." Finally, he said, "My motive for [having taken the] medical form of higher education is for letting me do what I want to do." By contrast, a pathologist who was formerly an academician but left the university to practice pathology in a private hospital, stated, "Work in pathology itself could be really deadly if it were not tied to active work in diagnosis." *

Here is another example of the academic pathologist's detachment from the decisiveness of the action-oriented world of the clinician. The surgical pathologist of one university hospital stated:

---

* It is not claimed that the pathologist's departure from his university is accounted for by his views on detachment from clinical work. But it does provide a contrast to the views of the physician who feels at home in the university where clinical participation is more limited from those of the physician who regards clinical participation as essential to maintaining his professional vitality.

> [This work is like that of] practicing pathologists—[but] I have a different attitude, I don't do it like an exact science . . . I don't like to be dogmatic . . . most surgeons [are] probably trained under dogmatism . . . [this] stifles thinking . . .

His emphasis is on deliberation and orderly reflection, the stock in trade of the researcher and scholar. Note that this love of contemplation is exhibited by a surgical pathologist, a man who must advise surgeons before and during operations on their immediate course of action.

Another ingredient in the academician's orientation is an interest in disease processes in preference to interest in patients. One academic pathologist stated that his interests are not primarily humanitarian. Another noted:

> . . . my basic interest is in disease rather than patients; my interests are more abstract than being a good clinician . . .

And

> . . . what I look forward to when I get up in the morning is seeing some disease . .

A third remarked:

> . . . autopsies here are not done primarily for diagnostic purposes, but for studying disease . . . we don't run a laboratory for the surgeons .

Here is another illustration. It is based on a discussion between a pathologist and the sociologist who was conducting the study:

> The university pathologist expressed concern over the fact that the pathologist often has access to the body of deceased patients too late, in view, especially, of the great speed of bacterial action. He pointed out that with the development of the electronmicroscope a delay of five minutes corresponds to a delay of five hundred years with the present microscope. He is, therefore, considering doing a provisional autopsy at the bedside, immediately upon evidence of death. The sociologist asked whether clinicians might be unfavorable to his proposal in light of responsibilities to members of the patient's family who might actually be nearby, as well as possible lack of certainty of death actually having occurred. The

pathologist stated that he had not considered these aspects; he acknowledged that when he was in general practice ". . . half the time I didn't know whether the patient was dead"—until later when very definite signs appeared.

Here, then, are orientations of the pure researcher that are rather alien to those of the clinical practitioner. They run counter to what is probably the most sacred ideal among clinical practitioners: the priority given to the treatment of the individual patient.

In the outlook of the university pathologist the preference for research on disease processes is doubtless valuable.* But the pathologist in the university is not only a researcher; he is also in interaction with physicians, within and outside the hospital, who look to him for collaboration in the treatment of specific patients. He is in the dilemma of having orientations of the pure researcher while being committed to participation in clinical practice.

This dilemma has repercussions in the academic pathologist's functions in recruitment and training of young pathologists. He is responsible for training practicing pathologists as well as producing new crops of academicians. It is noteworthy that the non-academic entrepreneurial and salaried pathologists indicated that their undergraduate medical exposure to pathology gave them little insight about *practicing* pathology. The entrepreneur stated, "In medical school the student does not find out what pathologists really do." Only the "entrepreneurial" of the three university departments of pathology offers, in the words of the chairman, "two types of training": training toward a career in research and training toward general practice of pathology. But here, also, there is preference for research. The chairman stated, "We try to interest our top boys in academic pathology." The chairman of another university pathology department stated that his chief purpose is to train pathologists for academic careers, that his department's task is "not primarily to train practicing pathologists, but teachers and investigators." Such adaptations are indeed liable to perpetuate the estrangements of pathologists, the academic as well as the nonacademic, from clinical medical practice.

---

* Additional academic orientations included interest in remaining a student ("One of the appeals of pathology is to continuously be a student" said one academic pathologist) and preference for teaching. The surgical pathologist at another university declared that he regards teaching to be his primary function.

In summary, university pathologists enjoy considerable autonomy in following nonclinical pursuits. This blends with the research-and-teaching emphasis of the academic milieu. But it is rather incongruous that clinically attuned practitioners are expected to be trained in this context. All this suggests that the graduates must expect a rocky road if they go into ordinary hospital practice. Their path will be easier if they remain in research settings.

Recapitulation: Autonomy and the Case of Medical Pathologists

It is not possible to say which of the arrangements for the practice of pathology has the greatest overall autonomy. Each enjoys autonomy in a different way. Each has emphasized autonomy in different areas of professional-social relationships. The emphasis on autonomy exists not only in verbal statements and in ideologies concerned with the need for autonomy, but in distinctive socially structured arrangements. Each type of practice consists of a configuration, a *Gestalt*, of working relationships and ideological commitments about the nature of professional medicine. Within each configuration there exist both distinctive areas of autonomy from, and distinctive areas of subservience to, the social environment. In its entirety each configuration is really a stand toward the social context in which the pathologist finds himself. It is a stand that emphasizes some aspects of professional medical practice and deemphasizes others. Each configuration can be seen as a system in fairly stable equilibrium with other external systems. Yet each configuration contains, internally, areas of flexibility. In this situation autonomy from and subservience to other systems are the "currency" in a process of exchange between systems. With these points in mind, let us review each type of practice again, looking first at the nonacademic pathologists.

The salaried pathologist has relatively little autonomy in administrative matters. He is decidedly subservient to the administrator of his hospital. This subservience provides him, however, with protection against the pressures from clinicians and his peers in pathology to get "more clinical" work arrangements, such as a fee system and financial control of the laboratory. In addition, the system allows him time to concentrate on substantive pathology, including research not bounded by immediate clinical needs.* For example, he does not have to deal with families of patients, and in his instruction of laboratory technicians he does not have to spend much time on the technical aspects of administrative control. In short, he enjoys considerable autonomy in pursuing traditional "pure" pathology, at a time when this is rather unpopular.

The fee-based pathologist is also subservient to administrative control, but less so than the salaried pathologist. The fee-based pathologist's official work arrangements are, essentially, equal to those of clinicians. His professional predisposition is toward clinical medicine; he places great importance on serving clinical needs efficiently and having good communications with clinicians. This stand implies great interdependence with clinicians: His income depends on the extent to which clinicians utilize his services; his conception of what pathology is emphasizes service to clinicians and, through them, to patients. He achieves the desired collaboration of clinicians through three mechanisms. First, he emphasizes the technical excellence of his services; in particular, he emphasizes that his test results are available quickly and that clinicians will have to wait a minimal length of time for them. In a sense this reduces his own autonomy in the technical realm for he cannot, as the salaried pathologist tries to do, ponder long over his work. Second, he makes extensive efforts to teach clinicians about the uses of, and recent developments in, pathology. To be sure the salaried pathologist teaches as well; but his effort is directed mainly to students and laboratory technicians. By emphasizing to clinicians how much they need pathology, the fee-based pathologist is in effect reducing *their* autonomy vis-à-vis the pathologist. Third, the fee-based pathologist has strong support from the hospital's administration, chiefly the chairman of the trustees, for his par-

* One day during the observation period this pathologist expressed great excitement over the fact that he had finally succeeded in diagnosing a particular piece of pathological tissue. He had been working on this sporadically for over a year and had consulted colleagues in different parts of the country. When success came, he shared the good news with the pathologists he had consulted. The fact that the patient whose tissue it was had already died several months before did not seem to dampen the pathologist's enthusiasm.

ticipation in clinical matters. Clinicians are obliged to make extensive use of his services, even when the findings may be unpleasant for themselves. Here subservience to the administration pays off in autonomy in relation to clinicians. This autonomy is shown in his ability to take a very active "policeman" role in order to reduce the amount of unnecessary surgery. In fact, the fee-based pathologist in the study initiated the hospital's arrangements for control of unnecessary surgery.

The entrepreneur pathologist is subject to little external, administrative control.* He owns his laboratory, bills patients directly, sets his own rates, decides his own work schedule. His conception of professional medical work includes all of these activities. He depends heavily on building up a personal clientele of patients and, more importantly, of clinicians. For instance, his daily work routine includes "making the rounds of doctors" among a coterie of doctors in order to see what need they have for his services. In the administrative sphere, then, he enjoys considerable autonomy. But in certain traditional spheres of pathology, namely, in the pursuit of research that does not have a direct clinical purpose or the control of unnecessary surgery, his arrangements permit him a very limited scope for participation.† In this kind of practice, autonomy in terms of administration is balanced against the need to solicit the good will of clinicians. But it must be noted that, given the high degree of interaction between the entrepreneur and clinicians, he is more likely to have influence upon clinicians than the pathologists who have little interaction with clinicians. This illustrates a paradox in social relations. A high rate of interaction has the potential for a high degree of dependence of members upon each other at the same time that there can be a high degree of influence upon each other.

Among academic pathologists, the entrepreneurial department has similarity to the arrangements of the nonacademic entre-

---

* He is not entirely free from external administrative controls because, in addition to owning his own laboratory, he visits and does work at several small hospitals. In each case he must take account of local hospital rules.
† In the hospitals in which he serves, his participation in policing activities is confined to "an advisory capacity" in the fact-finding stage. He does not take part in the policing activity itself. This contrasts with the fee-based pathologist's active leadership and the salaried pathologist's reluctant but active participation in these activities.

preneur. Here, too, there is a heavy emphasis on clinical participation and considerable autonomy in the administration of a laboratory. Both have organizational arrangements that are similar to those of clinical physicians. Among pathologists in the present study, the entrepreneurs have probably come farthest from the old second-class citizenship that pathology used to have within medicine. The academic entrepreneur has not had to pay the price of largely giving up policing, research and teaching tasks. Policing is carried out in university medical centers as part of the ordinary teaching program that involves most of the staff. The pathologist's participation does not cause him to be singled out as a "superordinate" and, therefore, does not endanger his colleague-ship with clinicians. In comparison with salaried academic pathologists, the entrepreneur has somewhat less time to spend on research and teaching in view of his administrative and clinical obligations. In sum, the academic entrepreneur appears to strike a fairly even balance for some autonomy in pursuing clinical as well as research, teaching, and policing functions. All this is facilitated by a high degree of economic independence from the hospital and university.

The salaried academicians, on the other hand, clearly de-emphasize their services to clinicians. This indicates considerable autonomy from pressures of clinicians and their practical world of day-to-day medical practice and is evidently facilitated by subservience to the administration of the university and its hospital. These pathologists do not determine their own salary or the budget of their laboratory or the size of their staff. They may influence these things, especially when they have research grants. But, administratively, they are under external controls. They are heavily immersed in the scholarly academic world, where autonomy to teach and to follow one's research interests is the basic objective and the basic reward.

NOTE **...**

1. See Fred E. Katz, "Analytic and Applied Sociologists: A Sociological Essay on a Dilemma in Sociology," *Sociology and Social Research*, 48, 4 (1964), 440–448.

Conclusion

While this book has emphasized autonomy as an important aspect of human social arrangements, it has deliberately underemphasized the psychological dimensions of autonomy—the processes by which *individuals* seek autonomy and their reasons for doing so. Instead, it has focused on the role of autonomy within social structures: how autonomy is incorporated in complex social organizations and what uses autonomy serves for these organizations. This book provides some theoretical models and some schematic illustrations of these processes; however, it does not claim to cover all processes involving socially structured autonomy. Indeed, it is hoped that this book will be a point of departure for many additional formulations.

Autonomy has been a subject of interest in studies by other sociologists, notably by Alvin W. Gouldner[1] and S. N. Eisenstadt.[2] The present book builds on their perspective by trying to place autonomy in an area of central concern for theorists. Deliberate focus on the potentials of one concept illustrates one of the uses of autonomy, namely, the scientist's prerogative of singlemindedly pursuing one insight by examining its relevance to many different contexts. As a strategy for developing a body of scientific knowledge, it holds the promise of bypassing the demand for explaining *everything* in a particular situation in favor of explaining *something* in many situations. Stated differently, it holds promise for developing generalizable abstract theory.

The theorist must be abstract—abstract enough to know that the business of science consists of building and testing abstract systems—but not so abstract that he becomes irrelevant to concrete reality. In this book the need for abstractness is given relatively full reign in Part I. In contrast, Part II demonstrates how autonomy manifests itself in concrete social situations. Here the picture of autonomy is less clearcut. Although the field study does not give a full ethnographic description of medical practice, it does provide enough detail to show that autonomy is embedded in a variety of other processes. It took some rather arbitrary acts of interpretation to highlight *autonomy* amid the variety of patterns that make up the concrete situations. Hopefully the interpretations are valid. But the arbitrariness of focusing on autonomy rather than, say, professionalization, illustrates the difficulty of developing theory inductively from raw concrete situations. To be sure, such situations can be handpicked to illustrate theoretical principles. But even then, analysis must rather arbitrarily focus on some features and minimize others.

This problem is not unique to sociological phenomena. The physicist would have difficulty deriving the principles of gravitation by watching the fall of a feather; a compact solid object will serve him much better. But in the ordinary concrete situation the fall of even a compact object will be affected by air currents, atmospheric conditions, the shape of the object, and so forth. Gravitation, by itself, will never be concretely perceived; it is an abstract formulation. One simply cannot get around the fact that the development of theory includes acts of arbitrary and abstract inventiveness. Yet the abstractness and arbitrariness of theory must not obscure the relevance of theory to real concrete situations. By including both analytic and field studies, we have tried to carry forward the work of developing theoretical sophistication in regard to autonomy while, at the same time, showing the problems involved as one looks at autonomy in its concrete manifestation.

We have implied that societies are inevitably limited in the extent to which they can exercise social control; after all, the absence of social control is what autonomy is all about. For the sociologist this means, in turn, that there are inexorable limits to his capacity to predict the details of social behavior. Is this a weakness? Not at all. Alfred North Whitehead long ago pointed out that young sciences tend to be unrealistically ambitious. Surely a science can gain momentum only when it recognizes its limitations. Or, stated as a hypothesis about autonomy, a discipline gains internal autonomy as it renounces some external autonomy.

NOTES ...

1. Alvin W. Gouldner, "Reciprocity and Autonomy in Functional Theory," *Symposium in Social Theory*, L. Gross (ed.) (Evanston: Row, Peterson, 1959), pp. 241–270; and "Organizational Analysis," *Sociology Today: Problems and Prospects*, Robert K. Merton, Leonard Broom, and L. S. Cottrell, Jr., eds. (New York: Basic Books, 1951).

2. S. N. Eisenstadt, *The Political Systems of Empires* (New York: Free Press, 1963).

Appendix

Two Quantitative Approaches to Autonomy

This section pursues the idea that there are limits to the interdependence of parts found in social organizations and that these limits —the autonomy of parts—can be stated quantitatively through the use of existing mathematical tools. Two mathematical approaches to quantification are given. Empirical translation is alluded to and nonquantitative applications have already been made by outlining necessary spheres of behavioral autonomy in schools and factories; but a systematic empirical effort remains a task for the future.

In attempting to specify the interdependence of parts of complex social organizations there are problems of practical research procedure in the construction of valid and reliable measuring instruments in order to make operational such concepts as power and authority, compliance and deviance. But before plunging into measurement problems it will be well to ask whether, even on theoretical grounds, there do not exist limitations to the interdependence of parts, and, further, whether one can formulate with precision these limits as elements of social systems.

Paying attention to *limitations* to the interdependence of parts of systems may seem to run counter to a recent movement in science. Organicists such as Walter B. Cannon[1] and Kurt Goldstein[2] have been influential in pointing to the interdependence of apparently different parts of systems, especially biological systems. They have justifiably received a hearing from social-system theorists. The physical sciences, too, generally state the properties of systems in terms of the

Prepared in collaboration with Justin C. Huang, Department of Physics, University of Missouri.

interdependence of parts or, more precisely, as the interdependence of variables in a system. But when dealing with actual systems, the existence of limitations to interdependence is evident in many instances. The engineer designing a machine deliberately allows for "tolerance" among the parts. He knows that if he were to specify each part's relation to other parts with infinite precision (assuming it were technically possible to build such a machine), the machine would not operate at high efficiency under normal conditions. For example, a wheel on a shaft that has no "play" would be unable to adapt to unforeseen conditions; a speck of dust on the shaft would bring it to a halt. But given a certain amount of play, the wheel can adapt to a variety of happenings (changes in atmospheric conditions, etc.) without impairing its services as a wheel. A degree of play, or indeterminance of the part in relation to other parts, can actually be useful for maximizing the contribution of the part to the system. This conscious building in of "play" differs from the view that, if the engineer could, he would design systems with infinite precision. The engineer designs machines to particular tolerance levels because no further precision is necessary for the purposes served by the particular machine. His actions are guided by the knowledge that economic and technical "costs" become prohibitive at certain points.[3] For practical purposes he attains higher efficiency under normal conditions by permitting some play in the parts.

The technical design of machines and the economic cost consideration may be thought of as illustrations of the basic premise of this discussion; that is, that structural and functional considerations set limits to how closely parts of systems should be specified. Two formal approaches to the specification of independence characteristics in social organizations will be offered. Our work has not progressed to the point where we can take the next step and fit existing data to the mathematical parameters in order to develop theorems about independence requirements for particular types of systems. For example, how much independence from control must hospital physicians have in order to perform optimally as medical practitioners, teachers of medical students, and hospital employees? Although a great deal of useful qualitative sociological literature on this type of problem exists,[4] clearly relevant quantitative data is not available at this time.

In the early sections of this book an attempt was made to clarify where, within complex social organizations, independence characteristics—that is, autonomy—must be found if the total organization is to achieve its mission. For schools, for example, spheres of teacher and pupil autonomy were delineated. The next step, obviously, is to try to develop techniques for quantitative analysis.

Quantification of Autonomy Requirements in Social Organizations[5]

Two sets of variables will be used to describe the state of a system. One class will be called set $A = \{A_h\} = \{A_1, A_2, \ldots\}$, where each element of the set $\{A_h\}$ corresponds to some observable, measurable characteristic of the system in question so that $\{A_h\}$ essentially defines the system. A_h's are all constants. They might include the number of levels in an administrative hierarchy, the size of departments, and so forth. The second class will be called set $X = \{X_i\} = \{X_1, X_2, X_3, \ldots, X_n\}$ where each element of the set $\{X_i\}$ corresponds to some observable characteristic of the system which can vary without destroying the identity of the system and that is not determinable from A.

Associated with the set X, one can define a third set

$$R = \{R_i\} = \{R_1, R_2, R_3, \ldots, R_n\}$$

where

$$R_i = \Delta X_i = X_i' - X_i$$

R_i, the element of the set, corresponds to the range in which the variable X_i can vary for some specified interval of time.

An attempt will be made to formulate the concept of the autonomy of a system using the above variables. Two approaches will be suggested.

1. *Autonomy defined as the number of independent decisions that a particular unit of a system can make.*

Let X_i represent the percentage of independent decisions that a system makes of type "i." Thus X_i will have a magnitude running from 0 to 100:

$0 =$ The system has no control over decisions
$100 =$ The system has total control over all decisions

The performance of a system will depend on the set of variables

$$\{X_1, X_2, X_3, \ldots, X_n\}$$

Let us represent the performance by a function P that is a function of variables belonging to set X:

$$P = P(X_1, X_2, X_3, \ldots, X_n)$$

Let us assume that P satisfies the necessary conditions of differentiability and convexity. If there exist constraints on our system, that is, if there exist relationships of the form $T_j(X_1, X_2, X_3, \ldots, X_n) = 0$ where j runs from 1 to m between our variables X_1, X_2, X_3, $\ldots$, X_n, then a set of generalized co-ordinates $Q_1, Q_2, \ldots, Q_{n-m}$ can be introduced that are linearly independent. The relationship between the old set $\{X_1, X_2, X_3, \ldots, X_n\}$ and the new set $\{Q_k\}$ is of the form

$$Q_k = S_k(X_1, X_2, X_3, \ldots, X_n)$$

where k runs from 1 to $n - m$. Our performance function can now be written in terms of the new set of variables:

$$P = P(Q_1, Q_2, \ldots, Q_{n-m})$$

We wish to maximize the performance of the system in a well-defined sense which need not be stated explicitly here. The condition that P be maximized is given by the set of equations

$$\frac{\partial P}{\partial Q_k} = 0 \qquad k = 1, 2, \ldots, n - m$$

The equations can be solved to obtain the values of Q_k's (and subsequently the X_i's) which will give the peak performance for the system. For simplicity, assume that no constraints exist and that the system depends on only two variables X_1 and X_2, then the convexity[6] conditions

$$\frac{\partial^2 P}{\partial X_1{}^2} \frac{\partial^2 P}{\partial X_2{}^2} - \left[\frac{\partial^2 P}{\partial X_1 \, \partial X_2}\right]^2 > 0 \quad \text{and} \quad \frac{\partial^2 P}{\partial X_1{}^2}, \frac{\partial^2 P}{\partial X_2{}^2} < 0$$

will ensure that $P(X_1, X_2)$ has a maximum and

$$\frac{\partial P(X_1, X_2)}{\partial X_1} = 0 \quad \text{and} \quad \frac{\partial P(X_1, X_2)}{\partial X_2} = 0$$

will be equations describing the maximum performance of our particular system. The solutions to the above equations will be $X_1 = X_{M_1}$

and $X_2 = X_{M_2}$. That is, a particular system will find that it gives a peak performance if the percentage of independent decisions that it makes is equal to X_{M_1} and X_{M_2}. Different social systems will of course have different values of X_{M_1} and X_{M_2}, since they will have different P functions.

It is convenient for generalization to other social systems to use the notation $P^A(X_1, X_2, X_3, \ldots, X_n)$ where A refers to set A, which essentially defines the system. It is hoped that different systems will have P functions of the same functional form but differing in the set $A = \{A_h\}$ of parameters used for the function $P^A(X_1, X_2, \ldots, X_n)$ The P function plays an all-important part in the analysis of social systems. Its functional form will have to await more experimental evidence. For our simple two-variable group it might have the form

$$P = aX_1^2 + bX_2^2 + cX_1X_2 + dX_1 + eX_2 + f$$

where a, b, c, d, e, and f are constants and form the set A of parameters, so that

$$\frac{\partial P}{\partial X_1} = 2aX_1 + cX_2 + d = 0$$

$$\frac{\partial P}{\partial X_2} = 2bX_2 + cX_1 + e = 0$$

and has the solution:

$$X_{M_1} = \frac{ec - 2db}{4ab - c^2} \quad \text{and} \quad X_{M_2} = \frac{dc - 2ae}{4ab - c^2}$$

These values give us peak performance.

What is the simplest X that can be chosen? For example:

$$X = \frac{\text{number of independent actions by the system}}{\text{total number of actions by the system}}$$

Of course, as a rule the analysis would be broken into different parts:

$$X_i = \frac{\text{number of independent actions of type ``}i\text{'' made by system}}{\text{total number of actions by system}}$$

Assuming no constraints, there would then be n equations to solve where $n =$ the number of elements in the set X_i. But this is simple if the equations are of linear form.

We have mentioned previously how constraints can be handled through the introduction of generalized coordinates. It can be han-

dled also through the use of Lagrangian Multipliers.[7] The function
formed is

$$L = P(X_1, X_2, \ldots, X_n) + \sum_{j=1}^{m} \lambda_j T_j(X_1, X_2, \ldots, X_n)$$

where the λ_j's are constants. Conditions for a maximum for the
$P(X_1, X_2, \ldots, X_n)$ function are now expressed by the following equations:

$$\frac{\partial L}{\partial X_i} = 0 \qquad i = 1, 2, 3, \ldots, n$$

These n equations together with the m equations of constraint

$$T_j(X_1, X_2, \ldots, X_n) = 0 \qquad j = 1, 2, 3, \ldots, m$$

give us $n + m$ equations in $n + m$ unknowns $(X_1, X_2, \ldots, X_n, \lambda_1, \lambda_2,$
$\ldots, \lambda_m)$. The solutions can be carried out in a straightforward manner.

So far only a single simple system has been considered. Now,
the task is to bring together many such systems to form a complex
organization. This complex organization will be described by a F function. F is some function of the $P^A(Q_1, Q_2, \ldots, Q_{n-m})$ functions described previously (now using generalized coordinates Q_k). Denoting
the $P^A(Q_k)$'s of using various subsystems by $P^\alpha, P^\beta, P^\gamma, \ldots$, the result
is $F = F(P^\alpha, P^\beta, P^\gamma, \ldots)$. The functional form of F will depend on the
internal forces that come into play between the various subsystems
within the organization. The necessary conditions for differentiability
and convexity will be assumed. The equations for maximizing F are
in the form

$$\frac{\partial F}{\partial Q_k{}^\alpha} = 0$$

where $Q_k{}^\alpha$ refers to the α subsystem and similar expressions for the
$\beta, \gamma, \delta, \ldots$ subsystems. The index k runs from 1 to $n - m$. The resulting
system of equations can again be solved in straightforward fashion.
If there exist constraints between Q_k variables of two or more subsystems, we can handle them by using similar techniques already discussed.

We can also offer a slightly different notion of autonomy:

2. Autonomy defined as a measure of how a particular social
system is unaffected by interaction with other systems.

For this notion of autonomy, X_i need not be restricted to be related to a scale representing a percentage of autonomy. It simply is a variable that is characteristic of how a particular system interacts with a different system. Two or more systems will again be denoted by their set A. Superscripts will denote different systems A^α, A^β, A^γ, . . ., and so forth. They will each have the set X and its corresponding R. Now attention should be given to the set A^α, which describes system α. As this system interacts with system β, they will be described by the two sets of variables $\{X_i^{\alpha\beta}\}$, $\{R_i^{\alpha\beta}\}$; superscripts are used to denote which systems are interacting. Next let system α interact with a third system γ. The variables used to describe this interaction will be $X_i^{\alpha\gamma}$, $R_i^{\alpha\gamma}$. For α interacting with system δ, the variable will be $X_i^{\alpha\delta}$, $R_i^{\alpha\delta}$, and so on for other systems. Compare sets $\{R_i^{\alpha\beta}\}$, $\{R_i^{\alpha\gamma}\}$, $\{R_i^{\alpha\delta}\}$, and so forth. If system α is largely unaffected by its environment, then $R_i^{\alpha\beta} \approx R_i^{\alpha\gamma} \approx R_i^{\alpha\delta}$ would be expected. If the system is easily controlled by its environment, then $R_i^{\alpha\beta} \gg R_i^{\alpha\gamma} \gg R_i^{\alpha\delta}$ might be expected, or other nonequal relationships. The set $\{\Delta R_i\}$ can then be used as a measure of autonomy where ΔR_i is the range that $R_i^{\alpha\beta}$, $R_i^{\alpha\gamma}$, and so forth cover. If $\{\Delta R_i\} \gg 0$; that is, if each element or many elements are much greater than zero, there is very little autonomy. As in autonomy of the first kind, the performance of a system can be represented by a function P, which is a function of the elements of the set $\{\Delta R_i\}$:

$$P = P(\Delta R_1, \Delta R_2, \ldots, \Delta R_n)$$

Maximum performance is then given by the expression

$$\frac{\partial P}{\partial(\Delta R_i)} = 0$$

The rest of the arguments are similar.

Discussion

We have concentrated on one variable, autonomy, in complex social organizations. It is postulated that this variable is intrinsic to these systems and has the characteristic of being specific and measurable even though, at the same time, it creates indeterminance within the system. We suggest that this holds for a class of social systems, namely, in-

ternally "differentiated systems." A plausible reason for the existence
of autonomy is that the central system cannot, in principle, account for
all the external forces acting on it. The flexibility given to its component units help to compensate for this lack of information. It is best
to illustrate this by the following figure:

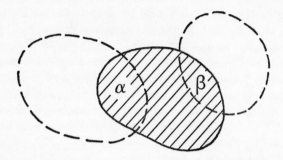

The central system (shaded area) contains α and β as units. Yet α
and β are both subject to external influences that affect their participation in the central system. However, the central system cannot,
as a rule, control the external influences that impinge on α and β;
this constitutes a lack of information for the central system.

In a sense, there exists a parallel in quantum physics if the intrinsic flexibilities of organizations are compared with the intrinsic
uncertainties of physical systems. These uncertainties exist because
the measurement devices in quantum physics are apt to alter the value
of the variable being measured in an unpredictable manner. One cannot isolate the measuring apparatus from the object being measured as
was the case for classical Newtonian physics. The physicist, however,
builds his theory around this difficulty by asking in his theories only
the probability of obtaining a particular value for a variable being
measured, when that variable is faced with the above difficulty of interference from the measuring apparatus. Put in more precise language,
the state of a physical system shows only the probability of obtaining
certain measurements. This can be summarized by saying that the
uncertainties of physics arise out of a lack of information connected
with the measurement process but that these uncertainties can be
specified in terms of probabilities. The present perspective proposes
that within social organizations there exist units that require a degree

of independence in order to play their part in these systems. The existence of these units creates a lack of information, and resultant uncertainties, for the systems. But the extent of independence of the units can, in principle, be specified and incorporated into the description of organizational structure. In both cases the lack of information leads to theory that allows for flexibility. In the case of quantum physics, one settles for relatively imprecise measurements. But the imprecision is largely overcome by the use of probability mathematics. In the sociology of complex organizations one accepts imprecisely defined structural units. But this can be overcome by a theory of organizations that precisely specifies the *limits* of independence.

The next step, obviously, is to apply more empirical substance to the theoretical statements. There exist efforts to measure discretion that come close to our interest in independent actions.[8] Elliott Jaques studied the frequency with which persons working in organizations have their work reviewed by superiors. On the basis of this and other techniques Jaques attempted to develop specifications for "equitable payment" for work done. This method comes close to measuring autonomy, but Jaques' interest in the psychological well-being of workers was somewhat different from our interest in optimal performance of social systems. Another approach might be to follow the lead of Mason Haire and categorize personnel on the basis of how they contribute to an organization.[9] Haire's work is essentially addressed to organizational survival. When applied to the present study, interest in survival would be combined with interest in task specialization. Thus organizations employing highly trained professionals—such as hospitals, universities, and research laboratories—would be expected to survive when the professionals enjoy a *particular* range of autonomy; below or above this range the organizations would be in jeopardy. At too low a level of autonomy the professionals become parochial "company men"; at too high a level their autonomy threatens loyalty to the organization to the extent that the organization's survival is at stake. Discovery of optimal autonomy levels for such organizations should be of interest to organization theorists as well as to practicing administrators. One would also expect to find distinctive autonomy characteristics associated with organizational size and administrative arrangements (e.g., relative autonomy at each hierarchical level) that are, in turn, related to organizational survival as well as to efficiency.

In any case, autonomy can surely be regarded as an ingredient of social structure. Hopefully these formulations will help to bring about further study, both qualitatively and *quantitatively*.

NOTES ...

1. Walter B. Cannon, *The Wisdom of the Body* (New York: Norton, 1932).
2. Kurt Goldstein, *The Organism* (Boston: Beacon Press, 1963).
3. The social counterpart to this is that when human activities are controlled closely there develop new "costs" that may get out of hand for those seeking to rule the organization. See Rensis Likert and Stanley E. Seashore, "Making Cost Control Work," *Harvard Business Review*, XLI (November–December 1963), 96–108. Likert and Seashore actually are less concerned with how closely human tasks are calculated than with the manner of introducing such calculations. But the degree-of-control problem may be inferred from their paper.
4. For instance, an entire issue of the *Administrative Science Quarterly* (June 1965) is devoted to "professionals in organizations." Several of the articles touch upon problems of constraint and freedom experienced by professionals.
5. Herbert A. Simon has used mathematical methods similar to those employed here. He deals, however, with different organizational phenomena. See Simon, *Models of Man—Social and Rational* (New York: Wiley, 1957), Chap. 10.
6. See L. Brand, *Advanced Calculus* (New York: Wiley, 1955), pp. 187–188.
7. *Ibid.*, p. 194.
8. Elliott Jaques, *Measurement of Responsibility* (London: Tavistock Publications, 1956).
9. Mason Haire, "Biological Models and Empirical Histories of Growth of Organizations," *Modern Organization Theory*, Mason Haire, ed. (New York: Wiley, 1959), pp. 272–306.

NAME INDEX

SUBJECT INDEX